Next

Next

The Road to the Good Society

Amitai Etzioni

BASIC
BOOKS

A Member of the Perseus Books Group

Copyright © 2001 by Amitai Etzioni

Published by Basic Books,
A Member of the Perseus Books Group

Designed by Elizabeth Lahey
Text Set in 11 point Caslon

Library of Congress Cataloging-in-Publication Data
Etzioni, Amitai.
    Next : the road to a good society / Amitai Etzioni.
    p. cm.
Includes bibliographical references and index.
ISBN 0-465-02090-9 (alk. paper)
    1. United States–Social conditions–1980– 2. United
States–Moral conditions–20th century. I. Title.

HN59.2 .E79   2001
306'.0973–dc21
                                                00-062116

FIRST EDITION

00 01 02 03 / 10 9 8 7 6 5 4 3 2 1

Love thy neighbor as thyself.

Lev. 19:18

Do to others whatever you would wish them
to do to you.

Matt. 7:12

Act in such a way that you treat humanity,
whether in your own person or in the person
of another, always at the same time as an end
and never simply as a means.

Immanuel Kant,
Grounding for the Metaphysics of Morals

Contents

Introduction

THIS BOOK IS FOR THOSE OF MY FELLOW CITIZENS WHO are tired of culture wars and hardened partisanship.[1] It is directed to those who do not believe that all truth or wisdom lies in one political camp and who do believe that we can work out a shared purpose and agenda. The book directly addresses the question of what must be done next–not merely by our national and local elected officials, but by our communities and, indeed, by ourselves.

A main thesis of this book is that center-based policies should involve much more than a compromise between Democrats and Republicans. We have learned over the last several decades that despite dominating so much of our public give-and-take and policy debates, the old opposition between statist liberalism and laissez-faire conservatism does not pay enough attention to a whole slew of issues. These all concern the body of society rather than either the state or the market; they concern our communities, culture, institutions, and values. These issues are often addressed (quite differently) by the religious right and by a new group of moderate thinkers (from which I hail) with the awkward title "communitarians."[2] This term, which draws on the concept of community, is hardly a household word, but it captures a new way of thinking about our societal issues.

It is a way of thinking that is centered around people convincing one another to be better than they would be otherwise, on having faith in faith, on persuasion rather than coercion, on what might be called "soft morality." (Communitarian morality is soft not because its tenets are weak but because its enforcement is communal rather than state driven.) Whether one favors a soft, hard, or neutral position on our societal issues, it is difficult to think seriously about our future without addressing the social, moral, political, and spiritual challenges that are staring us in the face.

The book addresses seven core questions that have one theme in common: How can we move toward a good society? The book opens with a brief exploration of what kind of society we ought to seek; this vision frames all that follows. The discussion then turns to the general direction in which we ought next to be moving. It presumes that our condition calls for neither a sharp left turn nor a drastic right turn. Instead, this discussion focuses on a major course correction within the centrist direction in which the country has been moving for more than a decade.[3]

The seven questions addressed are:

1. Instead of relying on either the government or the market, what ought we to do for one another as members of families, communities, and voluntary associations?
2. How are we to sort out which moral values should guide us, both as individuals and as communities? Can we avoid both moral anarchy and moral determinism by centering our lives around a moderate, soft moral-

ism–one that draws on persuasion rather than coercion?

3. What must be done to decriminalize and clean up politics, to shore up the rules of the game that we must follow to work out our differences? *What is to be done so that both major parties cease to put their own notions of misconduct above the voice of the electorate, thus becoming less inclined to drive from office future James Wrights, Newt Gingriches, and Bill Clintons?* Can campaign financing be thoroughly reformed, not by our current method of merely closing one floodgate as money gushes over and around the dam and everywhere else, but in a way that will stop the drift toward a plutocracy of one *dollar,* one vote?

4. Is our national unity threatened by increased diversity and inequality? And to the extent that such fissures are visible, what can be done to bridge the differences, to sustain unity, while maintaining a strong measure of multiculturalism? How can we respect our different heritages but still advance as one nation?

5. Does our vision for a good society at this stage require a further curtailing of government expenditures, regulations, and labor force, or has the time come for a more active state? Has the time come for a liberal course correction?

6. Are there ways to continue to grow a strong economy without endangering the social and moral values we hold dear? How can we continue invigorating the market–as economic conservatives favor–without letting it

overwhelm all other considerations, pushing us toward a twenty-four/seven society?

7. Last but not least: Are we out to become ever more affluent, or ought we aim higher? Beyond affluence, what?

●

In the days when ships were powered by sails, the French philosopher Montesquieu wrote that no wind will do for a ship that has no designated port. This book opens with the vision of a port: a good society of the sort that humanity has been aspiring to since the days of the ancient Greeks and the Old and New Testaments.

Much has been made in recent years of the quest for a civil society. Building a civil society is fully commendable, but it is not good enough.[4] The civil society is a narrow concept. The notion of civil society as it has evolved from Alexis de Tocqueville to Robert Putnam has at its core the image of a society endowed with a rich fabric of voluntary associations that protect the citizens from the state. And it is a society in which people deal with one another in a civil manner. The vision that beckons us is much more encompassing. We see a society that lives up to our basic moral values, to our conceptions of right and wrong. Granted, it is a shining city on a high hill. We may never reach it, but its lights ought to guide our climb.

Our journey starts where the recent presidential campaign left off. During the campaign, much was said about numerous specific programs. These included plans to increase literacy, protect us from OPEC, provide coverage for prescriptions for the elderly, institute smaller class sizes in our schools, and much else. This book goes beyond this laundry list, pointing to a set of principles with which to evaluate numerous current and future issues.

There is one particular sociological insight that underlies much of what follows. Namely, societies are like fully loaded barges that sit deep in the water and are difficult to steer. Often a course correction to one side will cause an oversteering in the opposite direction, requiring yet another change in course. We may be unable to advance in a straight line; changes in our natural and social environment, as well as new needs that arise internally, require frequent course adjustments. We can, though, stay the main course; the course corrections advocated herein aim to maintain the *general* direction we have been following for more than a decade.

Sometime around 1990 the Democrats discovered that if they wished to lead the country, they would have to move toward the center and ditch hard-core left-liberal positions, most notably those that clashed with core societal values of responsibility and opportunity.[5] During the Clinton administration, which was hardly cut entirely from one cloth, there were several grand showdowns between liberals and centrists, most of which the centrists won.

Republicans, too, changed course. They discovered in the mid-1990s that the country did not favor a conservative revolution. Most of the measures favored by the right were not enacted. And congressional Republicans increasingly worked out centrist policies with Clinton both before and after the 1998 impeachment hearings. During the 2000 election campaign,

George W. Bush moved the GOP further toward the political and philosophical center. At the end of the 1980s, demands for rights were very prominent. However, in the 1990s we learned to stress that individual rights go with social responsibilities. The slogan "Strong rights presume strong responsibilities" has gone from being a communitarian battle cry to almost a cliché, so widely has it been accepted.

I am not suggesting that because both parties are now basically centrist, no significant differences remain between them. One party rests on the liberal side of the center, the other on the conservative side. And one should realize that after the 2000 elections, both sides will move a bit away from dead center, back toward their respective corners. Still, the centrist positions of Bush and Gore highlight an undeniable fact–their national agendas are much closer to one another than to their respective left and right wings.[6] On numerous–albeit not all–issues, Gore's positions are much closer to those of Bush than to those of Ralph Nader, Louis Farrakhan, or Camille Paglia. And by and large, Bush's positions are closer to Gore's than to those of Pat Robertson or Pat Buchanan, not to mention David Duke.

The new centrist direction to which I have referred so far is sometimes labeled the "third way" because it avoids both the first way (the free market) and the second way (command-and-control economy, planned economy, or socialism).[7] Steve Goldsmith, the former mayor of Indianapolis, a moderate Republican, has referred to Bush's "compassionate conservatism" as the "fourth way."[8] (In a moment of levity I considered calling the centrist paradigm–which encompasses both Gore's and Bush's approaches–the seventh way.) But something is profoundly underplayed in most discussions of these third and fourth ways, and that is the role of community as it is broadly understood.

Public intellectuals, among whom I count myself, tend to write two kinds of books. One kind, scholarly ones, are aimed strictly at our colleagues. These tomes include technical terms ("jargon"), numerous footnotes, statistical and quantitative data, and other features of the academic apparatus.

The other kind of books we write are addressed to our fellow citizens. Here, we do draw on our and others' previous academic works and studies, but we try to write in English as unencumbered as a scholar can muster. We provide illustrative examples rather than detailed displays of data and technical analyses. Jargon is taboo. Open appeals to moral sense and good judgment are welcome. This book falls into the latter category.

One

The Good Society: First Principles

The Vision

WE NEED A CLEARER VISION OF WHERE THE CENTRIST way leads or in which direction we ought to pave it. Specific policies are welcome; technical details can be fascinating; there is room for debate about specific modifications required by this or that public program or legal structure. However, most people are not (nor do they seek to become) policy wonks or technocrats. Most yearn for an overarching picture of what we are trying to achieve, one that provides a framework for placing specific ideas, assessing specific past accomplishments, and planning for the future. We seek vision that inspires, compels, and gives meaning to our endeavors and sacrifices, to life.

Americans aspire to a society that is not merely civil but also good. A good society is one in which people treat one another as ends in

1

themselves and not merely as instruments, a society in which each person is shown full respect and dignity rather than being used and manipulated. It is a social world in which people treat one another as members of a community–a much extended family–rather than only as employees, traders, consumers, or even fellow citizens. In the philosopher Martin Buber's terms, a good society nourishes authentic, bonding I-Thou relations, although it recognizes the inevitability and significant role of instrumental I-It relations.[1]

Several core values that characterize a good society can be directly derived from its definition. On the face of it, child abuse, spousal abuse, violent crime in general, and, of course, civil and international war offend the first principle of treating people as ends. (Hence our love of peace.) For the same reason, violating individual autonomy, unless there are compelling public reasons, is incompatible with treating people as ends. This is the ultimate foundation of our commitment to liberty.

The ethical tenet that we should treat people as ends rather than only as means is far from novel, but this hardly makes it less compelling. Less widely accepted is the very significant sociological observation that it is in communities, not in the realm of the state nor the market, that this tenet is best realized. Hence, policies that undermine community distance the good society.

Single-minded ideologies seek to adhere to one overarching principle, such as according the needs of the nation priority over all else. In contrast, the centrist, communitarian approach often synthesizes principles that are in part incompatible by judiciously balancing two or more approaches.

The good society balances the state, the market, and the community. Much has already been made of the fact that the best way to proceed is to view government as neither the problem nor the solution but as one partner of the good society. Similarly, the good society views the market not as a source of all that is either good or evil but as a powerful engine that must be accorded sufficient space to do its work while also being carefully guarded.

And the government and the private sector tend to focus on our instrumental needs and thus foster I-It relationships. The community focuses on the social and moral needs and thus favors I-Thou relationships. Hence, moving toward a good society requires that these three sectors work together and keep each other in check. From this viewpoint, the question of whether we ought to have a free market is just as off the mark as the question of whether we should have a big government or—as Marx envisioned—a community without either. All are needed, but only in good measure.

Although the three partners differ in their views as to what their respective roles are and ought to be, it is essential for a good society that these three sectors seek to cooperate with and contain one another. Each partner can best help contain the other two, ensuring that none usurps the missions best accomplished by the other two and, in the process, maintaining the three-way balance that is at the essence of the good society.

The Road Ahead

I should acknowledge early in this exploration that the road map outlined here is fuzzy at the edges, somewhat vague, not fully etched. In effect, this is one of the main virtues of this approach: It points toward progress but is not doctrinaire or ideological; it is not a locked-in system.

The centrist way, followed here, has been depicted in negative terms—in terms of that which it is not. It has been characterized as a road neither paved by statist socialism nor undergirded by the neoliberalism of the free market. (Or even more succinctly, it tilts neither to the right nor to the left.) This book attempts to provide the centrist way with a positive and normative characterization as a public philosophy that both provides principles and points to public policy implications. Above all, it suggests changes people will have to introduce into their institutions and ways of conduct.

Is there one centrist approach, or are there multiple ways? Although some societies drive more in the left lane (e.g., France, Italy) and some more on the right side (e.g., the United States), the road they all travel is fully distinct from the one charted by totalitarian and libertarian approaches. Moreover, although the various societies differ in their specific synthesis of the ways of the state and the market, they are pulling somewhat closer to one another.

Given that each society has a distinct history and condition and that each started its journey from a different point, it stands to reason that each is moving in a different direction to find the best point of equilibrium between the state and the market. Most European societies still have to curtail the state further to allow markets to function effectively. Germany and above all France are still rather reliant on the big state. The United States may have overshot the point of balance, giving the market too much weight in recent years. The United Kingdom and Holland might be closer to the point of balance. And, to reiterate, all, too, have so far made short shrift of the third element of a well-balanced society: the role of communities.

Two

Giving Community
Its Due

The Neglected Partner

COMMUNITIES ARE THE MAIN SOCIAL ENTITIES THAT nurture ends-based (I-Thou) relationships, whereas the market is the realm of means-based (I-It) relationships. The state-citizen relationship also tends to be instrumental. True, some people bond at work and some barter in communities, but the main place ends-based relationships are found and nourished is in communities. As John Gray put it, "The flourishing of individuals presupposes strong and deep forms of common life."[1]

Communitarians, who stress the importance of community, often face the charge that community is a vague and elusive concept. (Note that other widely used concepts, such as class, elites, and even rationality, also resist precise definition.) Communities are based on two foundations, both of which reinforce I-Thou relationships. First, communities provide affective bonds that turn groups of people into social groups resembling extended families. Second, they transmit a shared moral culture from generation to generation, as well as constantly reformulating this moral framework over time. In effect, the presence of groupwide affective bonds and a shared moral culture is what defines and differentiates communities.

For those who see only two sectors, it is natural to assume or argue that if the government does something poorly, the private sector will do it well; if there are "market failures," the government can fix them. The fact is that there are hundreds of thousands of not-for-profits, voluntary associations, and other community-based organizations that often provide the best social services and cultural centers. Many of our best universities, hospitals, museums, orchestras, and social work agencies are neither public (governmental) nor private (profit making) but community based.

This third sector should be increasingly relied upon in the next years to shoulder a greater share of those social missions that must be undertaken, because communities can do so at a much lower public cost and with greater humanity than either the state or the market. In effect, *communities may well be the most important new source of such services in the foreseeable future, as the ability to increase taxes to pay for social services is nearly exhausted, and the total costs will continue to rise* at rates higher than inflation.[2]

Critics have argued that communities have largely disappeared from our landscape. Actually, communities have far from vanished even from our big cities, where they are often ethnically based.[3] We find them in Chinatown, Little Havana, Spanish Harlem, an Orthodox Jewish neighborhood in Brooklyn, and many hundreds of other such neighborhoods. And although in earlier eras, and to some extent today, communities have been largely residential (that is, membership was geographically defined, as in villages), now this is often not the case. Contemporary communities evolve among members of one profession working for the same institution (e.g., the physicians of a given hospital or the faculty of a college); among members of an ethnic or racial group even if dispersed among others (e.g., a Jewish community); among people who share a sexual orientation; and even among intellectuals.

By the definition of community followed here, and widely implied by other usages of the term, an interest group–a group of people who share an economic or political interest, say in pushing the government to allow exporting encryption or to provide subsidies to farmers–does not per se a community make. Interest groups have a much more limited scope, one based not on shared bonds and values but simply on interests. We already have a good term for them, namely, interest groups. Let communities stand out as a distinct category of social entities.

Communitarians have been challenged for viewing communities as a major partner of the good society; communities, critics point out, can turn oppressive and nasty. But so, most assuredly, can states and markets. The implicit methodology of the critics is to compare real social entities to unrealistically envisioned images of faultless places. Communities should be compared to states and to markets all as they exist today. Such a comparison will lead to the conclusion that underlies this endeavor: *Each of the three partners has its own strengths and weaknesses.* Each is best suited for some societal roles and not others. And–if society's work is properly divided among them–they can complement one another. Prodded by a free and vigilant press and an informed and active public, all three can be improved but hardly perfected.

The great capacity of communities to serve societal goals is highlighted by evidence that people who live in communities live longer, healthier, and more content lives than people who are bereft of such membership. Members of communities are also likely to have significantly fewer health problems than those who live in isolation. And with their desire for sociality well sated, community members are much less likely to join gangs, religious cults, or militias.

Many communities can discharge many social missions very effectively. Their actions cost the public little, and they can closely tailor their services to recipients because they know their members personally. Communities can play a major role in providing preventive and acute health care, reducing the need for publicly funded social services as divergent as child care, grief counseling, professional drug and alcohol abuse treatment, and law enforcement.

For all these reasons, cultivating communities where they exist, and helping them form where they have been lost, is essential for the future provision of much social good and should be a major priority of future progress.

Mutuality Beats Voluntarism

A good society relies more on mutuality than on voluntarism. Mutuality is a form of community relationship in which people help each other in a mutually beneficial way rather than merely helping those in need. Moreover, as Will Marshall, president of the Progressive Policy Institute, has stressed, mutuality applies not merely to one-on-one relationships but also to one-for-all and all-for-one kinds of relationships. As he put it, "Whenever possible, policies should be devised so that citizens who contribute to the community are rewarded, and those who benefit from the community give something back."[4] Neighborhood watch programs (in which neighbors agree to watch each other's property) and anticrime patrols (by community volunteers) are key examples of mutuality. So are consumer and producer cooperatives and mutual savings associations.

Forms of mutuality have always existed. Families, friends, neighbors, colleagues, and members of voluntary associations commonly practice mutuality. It is an important source of child care—for instance, in parent cooperatives, where parents provide a few hours of service each week, reducing public costs and providing natural, built-in staff accountability. Another good example is sick care, such as for people who are discharged "early" from hospitals and are helped by kin, friends, and other community members. When family and friends visit those who have lost loved ones, it is another example of mutuality.

Mutual help groups (oddly, often called "self-help groups") play a major role in helping people to cope with cancer, contagious diseases, alcoholism, obesity, and much else. They are a vastly underused resource. In the next years, the Centers for Disease Control and Prevention should greatly increase their efforts to highlight the value of such groups, as well as to help prime them and provide them with resources.

To ensure that mutuality is given as much support as its large-scale expansion requires, a cabinet-level Community Development Agency ought to be created, or such a division ought to be placed within the Housing and Urban Development or Health and Human Services agencies. The most effective option, however, may be to place such an agency within the White House Domestic Council. Whichever agency takes the lead in fostering mutuality, it must walk a thin line between providing for mutual help groups and discouraging these groups from learning to stand on their own feet.

Mutuality is undermined when treated as if it were based on an economic exchange of services. True mutuality is based on open-ended moral commitment. In mutual relationships, people do not keep ledgers, although they have a generalized expectation that the other will do his or her turn if and when their need will arise. Public policies and arrangements that attempt to organize mutuality as if it were an exchange may well end up undermining its moral foundation. Such policies include "time banks," in which hours spent babysitting (for example) are recorded, and the same amount of hours of voluntary service is expected in return. Similar programs include those in which used clothing is exchanged, and the amount of clothes one contributes determines the amount one can receive. Much looser and more informal arrangements are preferred because they are more compatible with communal relationships and do not smack of marketlike relations.

All this is not to suggest that voluntarism is unimportant for community building, civic spirit, and democratic government. Given that its roles have very often been spelled out, they need no discussion here. We should note, though, that whenever possible, voluntarism is best conducted as service learning. "Service learning" is a form of voluntarism in which those who serve do not act as if they are God's gift to mankind and instead acknowledge that they, too, benefit educationally and socially from their service experience. This form of service is especially compatible with the ideal of treating people as ends, although all forms of voluntarism are preferable to pure means-based relationships.

The question arises as to who will be able to provide for more mutuality and voluntarism in the near future as more and more women (formerly, a major source of both types of service) are gainfully employed. One new source should certainly be senior citizens, a rapidly growing class whose members live longer and healthier lives than their predecessors. In addition, they consume a growing proportion of societal resources and would benefit from staying actively involved in pro-social roles. Without this group's contribution, society may well be unable to attend to important portions of its social business. Civic Ventures is one of several organizations that runs some promising projects involving senior citizens. One of them is said to involve as many as 300,000 seniors.[5] There is much more civic gold in this vein.

All those who receive professional training that benefits from direct or indirect public funding, such as medical students, should be expected to provide some community service in return. Note that even those physicians who paid full tuition and board during their schooling cover only a fraction of the total costs involved in their training. In 1970, Congress established the National Health Services Corps (NHSC), which helped medical students pay for their education on the condition that they would work in medically underserved areas—rural or urban—for two to four years after graduation. In the first twenty years of the NHSC, more than 90 percent honored their commitment to serve; by 2000, more than 20,000 primary care physicians have been a part of the program. Unfortunately, the corps was virtually dismantled during the Reagan years.[6] It should be fully restored as soon as possible, and other health professionals as well as educators who benefited from the public till should be included.

Although all members of every community ought to be expected to contribute to the common good above and beyond that of their immediate communities, they should be allowed, indeed encouraged, to provide "extras" for their own communities. Communities should also be free to levy fees, dues, or taxes above and beyond those levied by the state. Parents should be welcomed when they contribute services, money, and assets to their children's schools rather than being expected to place all contributions into an anonymous pot to benefit all schools in a city or state. Ethically, it is asking too much heroism to expect people to be willing to do for one and all as much as they are willing to do for those close to them. And limiting contributions to "universal" ones, to those provided to all, is incompatible with a society that views communities as essential and constitutive social entities.

At the same time, more should be done over the next years to encourage affluent communities to reach out to less well-off ones. There is no contradiction between not forcing people to put all of their contributions into one pot and calling on them to share more of their affluence with the communities most in need. Given that there are currently few community-to-community programs, developing this form of intercommunity mutuality remains a challenge for both social thinkers and those who formulate social policies.

One must acknowledge that many sister city–like programs suffer some of the same limitations as voluntarism. Closer to mutuality are regional programs through which communities help one another to form joint arrangements ranging from sharing rapid transit systems to coordinating police efforts, from building highways and bridges to sharing an airport. These sharing arrangements are often quite properly touted as enhancing efficiency (indeed, many would not be possible without regional collaboration). However, they often–although by no means always–also serve as somewhat indirect forms of reallocating resources. (This is the case because better-off communities often pick up a larger share of the costs than the other communities. And at least in some cases, the less endowed communities reap a disproportionate part of the benefits generated.) To the extent that exhortation, persuasion, and highlighting the benefits of regional arguments for all involved do not suffice to promote greater regional mutuality, it might pay for state and federal governments to provide incentives for such programs to take hold, for instance, through matching funds.

Pro-Community Public Policies

The new administration would do well to launch a special review of all existing public policies and procedures that affect communities. It should seek to ensure that existing communities are not inadvertently undermined (e.g., by having their natural roles preempted) and that these policies and procedures opportune community development on a local, regional, and societal level. For example, usually, the more communities are involved in the decisions concerning how public funds are to be used, the greater the social payoff. For instance, citizens might set the hours a park is open and determine who may use it (dogs or children?) and for what purposes (public assembly or communing with nature?); and they might designate which streets will be turned into pedestrian areas. Asking such groups to assume some responsibility for maintaining shared facilities further enhances bonds among members.

The fact that members of the community will have to work out their priorities, in what might sometimes be a difficult process of give-and-take, is not a defect but a merit of this approach. In this way, public funds encourage communities to build and exercise their communal and civic muscles.

One can enhance community renewal by providing occasions for social gatherings (e.g., opening schools for community meetings or fostering neighborhood street festivals). Temporary organizers can be assigned to an area to initiate the formation of various social groups. And community renewal benefits from improvements to the physical conditions, safety, and accessibility of public spaces.[7]

New efforts to work more with communities must take into account that their boundaries do not often follow governmental ones. Such policies should, when possible, be tailored to communities' lines rather than attempting to make communities conform to preset administrative geographic boundaries. This is more readily achieved if the federal and state governments work directly with local community groups instead of only with local government agencies.

In recent years, much has been made of devolution, which is often interpreted as moving missions and funds from the federal to the state level, and in doing so, bringing power closer to the people. However, in many states the majority of people do not feel particularly close to the state capital or government. (For instance, many New Yorkers do not feel especially cozy toward Albany; nor do the citizens of Los Angeles and San Francisco look toward Sacramento to solve most of that which troubles them.)

True devolution reaches much further "down" than state government; it brings power to local governments, communities, and their member groups and associations. The further down devolution reaches, the more citizens are given opportunities to participate in their own governance. And to reiterate, the more politically engaged people become, the more effective their civic skills become, and the greater communities' efficacy becomes.[8]

As reliance on communities increases, policymakers had best take into account that communities need not be geographical or residential. Communities, for instance, can be formed around institutions (e.g., universities) or professions (e.g., longshoremen). They are often ethnically based and can even form in cyberspace (virtual communities).[9] Indeed, when communities that already share social bonds are further reinforced by providing them with access to a shared on-line "wired" space, the cohesiveness of the community is often strengthened.[10]

Even though communities need not be geographically based, many still are. Thriving communities often come together around core institutions such as schools, courthouses, and post offices. Hence, in principle, closing such institutions is detrimental to the approach advocated here. True, under some conditions, such as when an area has been largely depopulated, it might make sense to yield to considerations of economic and administrative efficiency and to consolidate or "regionalize" such institutions. However, such considerations of efficiency should never be considered the only relevant ones. To put it differently, a communitarian, centrist society gives much weight to social efficiencies by taking into account the human and social costs resulting from the loss of community when its core institutions are closed. Only when economic and administrative savings clearly outweigh social costs should core institutions–the mainstays of community–be closed.

A growing school of urban planning seeks to make the design of new developments (and the rebuilding of old ones) more community friendly. Among its leaders are Andres Duany, Elizabeth Plater-Zyberk, and Jeff Speck.[11] According to this school, future town planning and construction of buildings, streets, and neighborhoods are to take into account the enhancement of community. Among the numerous possibilities for doing so are wider sidewalks with porches abutting them and gates that block traffic but not pedestrians. One should note, though, that the art of community-friendly design has yet to be perfected, as we learned in places such as Reston, Virginia, Columbia, Maryland, and Celebration, Florida. Often, the results are not quite what either the planners or the members of the community involved had in mind–nor are the results necessarily fully supportive of community. Most important, any community design that actively attempts to build new communities will only affect our social conditions rather slowly. Much more attention hence has to be paid to designs that can shore up existing communities.

Much has been made in recent years of the role that faith-based groups can play in community building, especially in curbing antisocial behavior and in delivering social services. To cite but one piece of evidence: A study of a prison program run by a Christian group, the InnerChange Freedom Initiative, found that of 120 people who had been trained by the group and released from prison, only 15 have been rejailed, compared to 50 percent of those enrolled in other programs in the same state (Texas).[12]

Major proponents of recruiting faith-based groups in community service, often referred to as "Charitable Choice," include Senator Dan Coats (R.–Ind.), Senator John Ashcroft (R.–Mo.), and Steve Goldsmith, former mayor of Indianapolis, as well as Al Gore and George W. Bush.[13] Gore referred to faith-based groups as the middle ground between "hollow secularism and right wing religion";[14] Bush compared them to "a quiet river of goodness and kindness that cuts through stone."[15]

Even before Charitable Choice was enacted by Congress in 1996, significant proportions of the budgets for the social services of numerous religious groups were already drawn either directly or indirectly from public funds. Also, the First Amendment's separation of church and state–which is often interpreted as banning the allotment of public funds to religious institutions–is readily circumvented when payments due to individuals are in effect paid to religious institutions. For instance, hospitals, hospices, and nursing homes run by religious groups that frequently treat Medicare and Medicaid patients are often reimbursed by the government for providing these services. The same holds when the government pays denominational colleges for conducting research; such payments include not merely reimbursement for research costs but also funds for "overhead" that pay for other expenses of these institutions.

Relying more on faith-based groups and less on the government or the private sector is very much in line with the communitarian way of thinking. However, this should not blind us to two major dangers that lurk down this road, especially if ever more missions and funds are transferred to these groups: First, we shall soon learn that enrolling faith-based groups in large-scale social programs, while limiting their right to proselytize those enrolled in these programs, undermines their true nature and mission as more and more of their leadership, staff, and energy are absorbed by running these programs. Second, critics are sure to raise serious accountability issues that inevitably arise when public funds are used on a large scale by private groups.

Last but not least, there are obvious reasons for faith-based groups not to stick to the letter and perhaps the spirit of the legislation requiring them not to proselytize or engage in sectarian worship those enrolled in programs funded by the federal government. After all, these activities are the raison d'être for many of these organizations.[16]

In short, if excessive burdens are put on charitable choice, it will quickly lose its efficacy and public support. Faith-based groups can be a significant part of the communitarian way, but they are best kept as one of several carriers of social missions rather than made into the mainstay. All in good measure.

Enhancing Community Safety

Policies that seek to sustain or renew communities must take into account that communities are formed and reinforced largely in public spaces rather than in the privacy of people's homes. To the extent that these spaces are unsafe or depleted, communities are diminished. Therefore, communities should maintain public playgrounds, sidewalks, pedestrian walkways, parks, and plazas.

Public safety and community welfare benefit from the introduction of "thick" community policing, entailing much more than merely getting cops out of their cars to walk the beat. The community needs to be involved in setting priorities for the police and in overseeing their conduct, and the police should be involved in conflict resolution and in the protection of the overall quality of life.[17] There is no better example than community policing of an approach that both builds up communities and draws on them to mend the tear between state and society.[18] Reducing public cost is another bonus that often accompanies such policies.

To further protect children in public spaces such as playgrounds and neighborhood streets, local authorities should notify the members of whatever communities pedophiles move into after they have been released from jail. (Some such form of notification is required by the Megan's Laws that exist in all fifty states.) Such notifications cannot be avoided, because pedophiles are extremely difficult to cure and exhibit a very high tendency to reoffend. At the same time, communities should be warned against harassing these offenders; public education classes to this effect should be provided, as they are in the state of Washington.[19]

Finding ways to reintegrate former criminals into the social fabric of communities is a goal that should guide public policies in this area. For example, criminals who have paid their dues to society and lived legitimately without new arrests for, say, ten years should have their rights fully restored and their records sealed. Such records would be reopened only if they were reconvicted, before sentencing. In this way, a good society fosters repentance and leads to the full restoration of former criminals to membership in the community.[20]

Restorative justice, especially for nonviolent first-time offenders, serves the same purpose. This practice requires offenders to meet with their victims in the presence of third parties from the community. In the process, offenders learn about the victims' suffering, express their regrets, and make amends. The goal is to mix punishment with rehabilitation and to make amends to the victims while keeping these offenders as integrated members of the community.[21]

Much more can be done in this area. The preceding examples illustrate the communitarian approach to community building rather than providing an exhaustive catalog of such programs.

Three

For a Soft Moral Culture

IN THE 1950S AMERICAN SOCIETY HAD A STRONG AND
clear set of social values, but these were somewhat authoritarian, unfair to women, and discriminatory toward minorities. These values
were roundly attacked by the civil rights movement, the counterculture, and the women's rights movement, among others. Although
these movements opened America's eyes to the negative practices of
its own society, these attacks caused a moral vacuum, typified by unbounded relativism, situational ethics, and excessive individualism.[1]
Liberals were reluctant to step in to fill the void and to help evolve a
new moral culture.[2] Social conservatives, especially the religious
right, have viewed a return to traditional morality as the key to national salvation. They seek to rely on the state to enforce good behavior. Thus they desire to ban divorce, mandate prayer in public
schools, roll back the gains of gays and women, outlaw abortion, and
require the teaching of creationism.

The great and growing American center has become increasingly uncomfortable with these ultraconservative, theocratic positions. During the 1990s, the religious right has lost a great deal of its political clout. But the moral vacuum it sought to fill has continued to gnaw at us. In response, a group of new communitarian thinkers (for whom I sometimes speak) seeks to provide a different approach to moral issues by drawing new, shared moral understandings, drawn from moral dialogues, rather than by relying on hierarchical dictates. The approach emphasizes convincing people to change their ways rather than enacting coercive laws to force them to do so. To put it more bluntly: We can no longer shy away from addressing the issues the right wing and the social conservatives have raised, but we ought to address them in a rather different manner than they advocate.

The different ways American society dealt with addiction in the 1920s and in the 1990s illustrate the profound difference between social conservative and communitarian approaches. Prohibition was imposed from above, with little public participation in the decision, and it was a disaster. The ban on smoking in public spaces, in contrast, followed a wide consensus, can rely almost completely on voluntary compliance, and is almost a total success. I am referring to this kind of moral culture, based on dialogue and persuasion, as *soft morality*. Its tenets are not soft, but its way of fostering them is.

The Power of the Moral Culture

When we consider the current and prospective importance of communities, we are often inclined to focus more on the interpersonal bonding and mutuality they provide than on their role in formulating and fostering moral culture. However, both elements of community have an important role in nourishing I-Thou relationships and in fulfilling important social missions. True, community bonding is a major source for satisfying a profound human need for affective relationships with others. But in addition, the community's moral culture maintains social order, without which a good society is inconceivable, and it does so with minimal state intervention in social behavior.

There are some forms of behavior that a good society considers anathema and must seek to curb (e.g., damaging the environment, domestic violence, child abuse and neglect). It is a community's moral culture that helps to curb such behaviors. The community's ability to draw on subtle and informal social regulating processes, such as approbation and censure, is much more compatible with ends-based relations than is relying on the coercive powers of the state.

Extensive studies have repeatedly demonstrated that informal social regulating processes play a major role in curtailing drug abuse, preventing petty crime and violations of the environment, and heading off many other antisocial behaviors.[3] The community can also foster good conduct, such as attending to one's children and elders, paying taxes, and volunteering.

Strong evidence in support of the virtue of community life is found in religious communities. Practically all kinds of antisocial behavior are relatively low in Mormon communities in Utah, Orthodox Jewish communities in New York, and Black Muslim groups. They are also lower, on average, in villages and small-town America as compared to large cities, where communities are less prevalent.

The value of communities is further highlighted by the finding that *people who live in communities live longer, healthier, and more contented lives* than those bereft of such membership. Community members are especially likely to have significantly fewer psychosomatic illnesses and mental health problems than those who live in isolation. Studies in natural settings have found that persons subject to social isolation suffer in a variety of ways, both physical and mental. For instance, researchers concluded that "socially-isolated men have nearly double the mortality from cardiovascular disease of those with the largest social networks."[4] The risk of a recurring cardiovascular event is also heightened by weak social bonds, according to the same study.

The fact that social isolation is dangerous for mental health was highlighted in 1955 during the first mission to establish a U.S. base in Antarctica, where isolation caused paranoid psychosis.[5] Since then, numerous studies have shown that isolation significantly increases various psychological health risks.[6] In their classic study of New Yorkers lonely in high-rise apartments, *Mental Health in the Metropolis*, Leo Srole and his associates found that 60 percent of the residents had subclinical psychiatric conditions and 20 percent were judged psychologically impaired.[7] Other studies have repeatedly demonstrated that after work-related stress, the most important social factor in mental health is marital, familial, and friendship relationships.[8] Elderly people who live alone, have no friends, or have poor relationships with their children are 60 percent more likely to develop dementia than those whose social contacts are more satisfying, according to a study published in the medical journal *The Lancet*.[9]

In 1988, Wellsburg, West Virginia, had a particularly high incidence of heart disease—29 percent above the national average. By 1996, the community's cardiovascular health profile was among the best in the state, according to a study conducted by Mary Lou Hurley and Lisa Schiff.[10] The improvement is reported to be largely the result of community-organized walks, healthy potluck suppers, and numerous classes in aerobics and on ways to reduce cholesterol, blood pressure, and stress.[11] The 1996 screening of 182 community members found that they had maintained their weight loss and most of their reductions in cholesterol and blood pressure.[12] According to the researchers, "The average wellness score . . . topped the 1988 baseline by 12 percent and the average fitness score by 42 percent."[13]

There are scores upon scores of studies with findings of the following kind. They highlight the effects of communal bonds and their merit in curbing antisocial behavior.

- Volunteer patrols called Orange Hats chased drug dealers out of their neighborhood in Washington, D.C. In the process, members of the community also became closer to one another. And when these drug dealers moved to other communities, they faced a similar fate, which disrupted their markets.[14]

- In the county of Tillamook, Oregon, community efforts resulting from the collaboration of different groups, including religious and liberal organizations, led to a decrease in teen pregnancy rates from twenty-four pregnancies per thousand girls age ten to seventeen in 1990 to seven per thousand in 1994.[15]

- Crime of every kind, violent and nonviolent, is much higher in urban America than in small towns and villages. For instance, violent crime (which includes murder, rape, robbery, and aggravated assault) takes place at a rate of 1,287 annual offenses per 100,000 inhabitants in cities of 1 million and over, while in cities of 10,000 and under, the violent crime rate is 397. Even rape–a crime with one of the smallest differentials–still takes place at a rate of 28 per 100,000 inhabitants in towns of less than 10,000, as compared to 37 for cities with a million or more.[16]

A special commission should conduct a review of most existing public policies to determine whether the renewal and maintenance of existing communities are not being inadvertently undermined, and how such policies might be reformed if they are indeed hampering communities from carrying out their natural roles. Furthermore, the same policies ought to be examined to establish whether they positively opportune community development on the local, regional, and societal level.

Centrist governments do best when they resist the rush to legislate good behavior. When there is a valid need to modify behavior (say, to encourage saving water during a drought), the state should realize that relying on informal, community-based processes (members chiding each other and appreciating certain forms of conduct) is preferable to relying on the law. Legislation numbs the moral conscience. When legislation is introduced in places where a moral culture *does* exist, the result is often to diminish the moral voices of the community. For instance, if the government were to rule that alcoholics must attend Alcoholics Anonymous meetings or face jail sentences, such meetings would be far less effective than those in which attendees participate because of their own inner motivations and the encouragement of those close to them.

We have also learned from government attempts to suppress divorce and alcohol consumption that such policies tend to fail. One should have faith in faith. The shortest line leading to "good" conduct, whatever one considers such conduct to be, is convincing people of the merits of the moral claims we lay on them. To provide but one example of where the suggested communitarian principle should be applied: Some of the twenty states that are trying to shore up marriages by making divorce more difficult should instead consider relying on moral dialogues, which would lead the community to form a culture and conditions supportive to families. Law enforcement should be the last resort and not the first line of defense.

Limiting the Power of Communities

Even though the moral cultures of communities make significant contributions to good societies, community-based morality does need to be judged. We cannot assume that the values around which communities form will necessarily meet whatever moral criteria we might bring to bear when assessing the moral standing of these values. At first blush, values may seem good per se, and some do use the term this way. However, there are errant values—for instance, the beliefs held by anarchists—as well as values that we judge to meet our criteria for goodness, for virtue. Where can one find such criteria?

One way to proceed is to assess the community's moral culture by drawing on shared societal values that are ensconced in the basic laws or in the constitution. This is especially true when it comes to the individual rights that no community should be free to violate. That is, communities, just like each of the other elements that contribute to a good society, must be contained.

Because communities have oppressed individuals and minorities, particularly in earlier ages, it is the role of the state to protect the individual rights of all community members, as well as those of outsiders present within the communities' confines. Thus, no community should be allowed to violate anyone's right to free speech, right to assembly, or any other constitutional right. Any notion that communities can be relied upon as the sole or final arbitrator of morality need only look at those twentieth-century southern communities that reached a consensus on lynching people on the basis of race.

Although the question of where to draw specific community restrictions is open to discussion, in principle, no community can be relied upon fully to determine right and wrong. Should immigrant communities with traditions of arranged marriages be allowed to continue this practice in cases in which consent is dubious? Should female circumcision or child labor be tolerated? These are examples of the kind of questions over which communities should not have the final say, as they concern basic rights.

This vision of contained yet thriving communities is not without precedent. Many communities within democratic societies abide by the larger entities' constitutions or basic laws. Members of kibbutzim have strong conceptions of what is expected of members of their respective communities, but at the same time, no one is denied the right to free speech, assembly, and so on. Although local conceptions of social order and individual rights occasionally clash in American suburban and professional communities, both are usually honored.

In a good society, the rules that contain communities may be further extended, but the basic principle is the same: Unfettered communities are no better than unfettered markets or states. To reiterate: At the core of a good society is a balance achieved by mutual containment, and the community is not exempted. However, the fact that communities can get out of hand should not be used as an argument against communities per se. Like medicine, food, and drink, communities are essential elements of the good life if taken in good measure, but if taken to excess, they can destroy it.

Rights and Responsibilities

A good society combines respect for individual rights with the expectation that members will live up to their own responsibilities to those near and dear to them as well as to the community at large. One of the greatest achievements of the communitarian approach has been curbing the language of rights, some of which had turned every want and interest into a legal entitlement and fostered unnecessary litigiousness. "Rights talk," which led to a disregard of social responsibility, was dominant in the 1980s, the days of rampant individualism. By now it has been largely replaced by a wide recognition that both individual rights and social responsibilities must be respected.[17]

Basic individual rights are inalienable, just as one's social obligations cannot be denied. However, it is a grave moral error to argue that there are "no rights without responsibilities" or vice versa.[18] Thus, people who evade taxes, neglect their children, or fail to live up to their social responsibilities in some other way are still entitled to a fair trial, free speech, and other basic rights. There may be fewer rights than some would claim, but our constitutionally protected rights are not conditional. We cannot and should not be required to do anything to "earn" them. Hence, policies that deny criminals the right to vote while jailed–or in some cases, even after they have served their terms–should be modified. Following the same principle, nobody should be denied the basic necessities of life even if they have not lived up to their responsibilities–for example, finding work. Society can show its disapproval and punish irresponsible individuals without disenfranchising them or condemning them to abject poverty.

At the same time, a person whose rights have been curbed (say, someone who has been denied the right to vote because of a registration foul-up or a jail sentence or who has been silenced by a meritless libel suit) is still not exempt from attending to his or her children, not littering, and performing other social responsibilities.

We cannot emphasize enough the core tenet of the good society: that people must assume responsibility for others. No one is exempt from this expectation, although of course individuals vary greatly in the contributions they can make. In considering this matter, a mental experiment may help: Consider a paraplegic who has lost the use of his limbs and is permanently institutionalized. He uses a small stick in his mouth to turn the pages of a book. Should we provide him with a nurse's aide to turn the pages, or should we expect him to take that much responsibility for his own well-being? In order both to respect the person's dignity and to remain in line with the expectation that everyone should do as much for the common good as they can, we would expect the paraplegic to turn the pages himself (assuming he can do so without undue effort). If assuming responsibility to the best of one's abilities applies under these circumstances, surely no one is exempt from contributing to the common good in line with his or her ability.

Accordingly, high school students should be encouraged to do community service as part of their civic practice.[19] Senior citizens should be expected to help each other, members of their families, and their community. (Likewise, those who receive welfare and cannot find gainful work should hold community jobs.) People with contagious diseases should be expected to do their best not to expose others, and so on.

The reference here is not primarily to legal commitments, enforced by courts and by the police, but to moral expectations. Discharging one's responsibility should not be considered a sacrifice or a punishment but an ennobling activity, something good that people do. Indeed, high school students can gain a deep satisfaction from working in soup kitchens, as senior citizens can by volunteering to run social centers for other seniors, and so on.

Responsibility *from all* is to be paralleled by responsibility *for all*. That is, communities in a good society assume a moral responsibility for ensuring that no one is treated inhumanely, which occurs when they are denied the basic necessities of life. Voluntary associations, extended families, friends, mutual savings associations, and religious charities can carry part of this burden. Given that communities may be overwhelmed by needs, especially following war or natural disasters, the final responsibility to ensure that all are attended to falls on the state.

Communities can play an especially important role in ensuring that everyone is included and treated with full respect, as an end in themselves.[20] (As Philip Selznick put it, "All persons have the same intrinsic worth. . . . Everyone who is a person is equally an object of moral concern."[21] This is the essence of justice. Selznick adds that the most important threat to social justice is social subordination. Hence, social power should be "dispersed and balanced" but not wiped out.[22]) An obvious example is to ensure that no one will be subject to discrimination based on race, ethnicity, gender, sexual preference, religious background, or disability. Discrimination, which generates humiliation, breeds hate, and sets people against people, not only violates our elementary sense of justice but is also incompatible with treating people as ends in themselves. Here, too, the state must be the ultimate guardian against mistreatment.

All policies that impinge on the balance between individual rights and social responsibilities should be reviewed and adjusted accordingly. The right to privacy, for example, is to be respected, but it should not take priority over protection of life and limb. For instance, mandatory drug testing of school bus drivers, train engineers, and air traffic controllers is legitimate because in these cases, the violation of privacy is small whereas the danger to those whose lives such people are *directly* responsible for is considerable. After all, although the Fourth Amendment dictates that there be no unreasonable search and seizure, it does not ban searches altogether. And reasonable searches have long been considered acceptable if there is a strong public interest. It is hard to imagine a greater public interest than a bus full of children or a train full of people. (Indeed, in these cases, courts by and large have allowed mandatory drug testing to continue.) Some other professions and occupations that meet the same criteria might well be included (for instance, pilots), but there is no compelling public interest in testing most people. In contrast, violations of the privacy of our medical records, which concern the most intimate parts of our lives and yield at best minimal social benefits, should summarily be banned.[23]

Much attention has been paid in recent years to the social and moral effects of the Internet, of the expanding cyberspace. These pale in comparison to the challenges posed by the biotech revolution arriving close on the heels of the digital one, and by the combination of these two developments. As science and technology advance, we must work especially diligently to protect our values and to develop the institutions that allow us to do so. Since the beginning of the industrial revolution, the development of social and moral institutions has lagged behind technical and economic developments. In recent years, this gap has widened. New technological developments focus our attention on this challenge. A society focused on ends-based relationships cannot exist unless we pay far more attention to this matter. Bioethics commissions and research centers have but scratched the surface of these issues, which require urgent study, deliberation, and moral dialogues on a vastly larger scale.

Moral Dialogues: Changing Moral Cultures

Debates about our moral culture are often unnecessarily polarized. We are not limited to either adhering to traditional social structures and mores (e.g., traditional family with two parents, mother at home) or treating all such as if they had equal legitimacy, as "lifestyle options" (e.g., two parents, single parents, gay marriages, serial monogamy, polygamy). For instance, a community can express a preference for peer marriages, in which both partners have the same rights and responsibilities, without condemning other forms of family. The point is not that peer marriages are necessarily the best family structure but that there are social and moral options between rigidly sticking to tradition (as parts of the religious right demand) and asserting that anything goes (as some on the left hold). The discussion turns next to how communities sort out these issues in well-balanced societies.

Although the moral culture of a given community or community of communities is in part handed down from generation to generation, it is by no means fixed or "traditional." On the contrary, community morality is continually recast in line with new social needs, demands, insights, and above all, moral claims. This recasting occurs through a process of special importance to the good society: moral dialogues. Moral dialogues are composed of a large number of hours spent over meals, at bars, in car pools, at work, and in the media (e.g., call-in shows) on one "hot" moral issue.

Local communities, whole national societies, and sometimes even people in many nations are engaged in extensive dialogues about one or more acute specific moral issues. These include such rather general subjects as our moral duty toward the environment, women's rights, and sexual discrimination and relatively more specific issues such as gay marriage, putting a child on trial as an adult, or DNA testing of a whole village to find a suspect (as was done in Britain).

Usually only one or two topics are the subject of intensive moral dialogue at any time. Anyone can try to initiate a moral dialogue, from the president to a local poet, from a media personality to a group of protesters. However, it is the public at large that decides which few of the many thousands of attempts to initiate a moral dialogue win an audience.

Despite claims to the contrary, the media—which serve as important venues for moral dialogues—control neither the agenda nor the outcome, although they of course influence both. This is in part because the media themselves are not of one mind, and in part because the public is much less susceptible to brainwashing than has often been assumed. To test this observation, analyze any moral dialogue—for instance, about the death penalty. By and large, the major media are much more opposed to the death penalty than the majority of the public, but the public is not swayed.

Moral dialogues are largely not about facts; rather, they are about values. These are dialogues among citizens rather than among experts. This does not mean that there is no room for factual arguments or that these have no effect. The arguments, though, are for the most part not empirical but ethical in nature. Review, for instance, the arguments about whether or not we should have bombed Serbia during the Kosovo war or whether we should allow gay marriage. The subject of moral dialogues is moral cultures, and it is these that such dialogues seek to reformulate.

When a community is engaged in a dialogue on what is right, the discussion often seems disorderly, meandering, and endless. However, it often does lead to a recasting of that community's moral culture—of what the community appreciates or censures—and to new shared moral understandings.

Most important, people often modify their conduct in the process, without changes in public policy, law, or policing. Indeed, there may be no other way to change the behavior of a large number of people without using a large amount of force or incurring huge economic costs. For example, in the 1950s most communities had no sense of a moral obligation toward the environment. A profound moral dialogue that developed in the 1960s led not merely to a new shared moral sense of our duty to Mother Earth (although communities continue to differ on what exactly that entails) but also to a fair amount of changed behavior, such as voluntary recycling and conservation of energy. In short, *if a community needs to change its social policies in a significant way, such changes are best preceded (as far as public policies are concerned) and largely generated (as far as changes in personal and social conduct are concerned) by moral dialogues.*

One should grant that involving the public in a moral dialogue about a major change in public policy, especially those that concern moral and social issues, makes it more difficult to govern. These dialogues consume time and do not necessarily end up where the government may wish to go. But at the same time, there is no question that without such dialogues it is not possible to achieve profound and encompassing changes in the way a society conducts itself in moral and social matters. In short, moral dialogues are the most important engine of significant change in a society aspiring to be good.

Family: A Need for a Definitive New Look

Throughout history, in all societies, families have been entrusted with initiating character formation and introducing the moral culture to the next generation of the community. We now face the question of whether children can be well educated (in the deepest sense of the term) from the youngest age by single parents or in child-care centers. It is an unfinished debate.

Before we can settle any of the numerous specific issues that arise from the transition from the traditional to the postmodern family, we require a more conclusive examination of the evidence about the effects of various child-care patterns at home and in institutions. The White House, the Department of Health and Human Services, or an independent body, such as the National Academy of Sciences, should convene a "science court,"[24] composed of top social scientists. The "court" would hold public hearings and interrogate scientific witnesses and representatives of the various bodies of thought on the subject of child care. The court might require additional analysis of existing data or the generation of new data to provide a strong and shared body of relevant evidence. It should seek to reach solid, credible conclusions about critical issues that arise concerning our ability to replace the two-parent family.

Such a "court," the National Reading Panel (which included educators, researchers, and parents), worked to sort out the information about the relative merits of various methods of teaching children to read, seeking to end the so-called reading wars.[25] The panel released its findings in April 2000, and it is still unclear how widely they will be accepted. Nonetheless, this illustrates how such science courts work.

Clearly, it makes a great deal of difference for the moral culture and public policy whether children suffer greatly or actually benefit, as some maintain, from new forms of family arrangements and the institutionalization of children. The science court's conclusions would focus, feed, and accelerate moral dialogues on the issues at hand as well as provide a major source for policymaking, but it should have no enforcement powers. The science court should focus on young children, especially from birth until age five, because these are the years in which the foundations of character are formed.

The science court should investigate not merely whether the absence of a second parent is harmful but also whether there is a growing "children deficit" and, if so, its implications. There is growing evidence that the birthrate in several developed societies is falling below the replacement rate (the number of adults who die each year exceeds the number of children born needed to replace them) with considerable negative consequences for those societies. The most important of these consequences is that an ever smaller number of workers must provide for an ever increasing number of older retirees (and other dependents). (Such a population shortfall can be ameliorated by a high level of immigration, but that creates a host of issues all by itself.) To put it more sharply, if we once held that the first social duty of the family was the moral education of children, we may now have to say that duty calls for having children at all. Of course, one must stress that no stigma should be attached to families who cannot have children or who see themselves as psychologically ill-qualified to raise them. But the notions that children are a burden, interfere with careers and leisure time, and are "inconvenient" are simply more reflections of radical individualism and Sisyphean materialism. Neither is compatible with a good society.

The introduction of new family policies might best be delayed until the work of the court is completed. This holds, for instance, for various suggestions that have been made regarding new forms of marriage, including asking a couple to commit to an unwanted marriage until their children reach a given age, raising the age at which people can get married, providing additional legal protections to domestic partnerships, and putting new restrictions on divorce.

No such moratorium is necessary on the introduction of so-called covenant marriages, because they merely facilitate behavior and do not mandate it. This form of marriage, introduced in Louisiana, affords couples the opportunity to bind themselves voluntarily to a higher level of commitment. Couples agree to participate in *pre*marital counseling, and counseling while married, if one spouse requests it, and to delay divorce for two years if one partner files for it, except in cases where a crime has been committed.

Some family matters can be taken for granted and require no study or hearing. There should be no return to "traditional" forms of family, in which women were treated as second-class citizens; such a turn would violate the principle of treating all as ends in themselves. Fathers and mothers should be assumed to have the same rights and responsibilities. Fathers are obviously capable of child care, and women clearly work outside the home. The current law that allows parents–mothers or fathers–of newborn children to take unpaid leave should be changed to provide paid leave, gradually extending the length of the leave. The law should encompass corporations of all sizes and not merely those that employ fifty or more workers (as is currently the case). (The use of unemployment benefits to pay new parents is under active consideration in some fifteen states.) Furthermore, the law should ensure that workers returning from family leave will either find their jobs waiting for a given number of years (as is the case in several European societies) or be provided with training for a new job at public expense.

There is no one correct way to balance work and family; each person and couple must work this out. It is, however, in the interest of a good society to encourage and enable parents to spend more time with their children.

Much more should be done in the near future to make it possible for people to engage in gainful work at home. Tax incentives for corporations that facilitate telecommuting might help. Working at home has clear benefits for the family and the environment (not to mention rush-hour traffic). Such work does encounter problems, problems that have been familiar since the days of the early looms. For example, how do we foster work at home without inadvertently undermining working conditions, or even safety? These are matters that should be worked out in the near future to reduce the conflict between work and family.

All these steps are of merit in and of themselves. They also send a message: A good society cares profoundly about children.

Schools: Beyond Teaching

Much has been written about making schools into more effective tools for the information-based, competitive economy and about the need to raise the level of academic skills and knowledge of our graduates. However, we have known about the importance of character development since Aristotle. In our society, schools are where the character of young people is developed, even if such development was not neglected at home (and especially if it was). Schools are places where people ought to learn how to treat one another as ends rather than only as instruments.

Currently, only a minority of public schools have civic education courses, and even fewer have character development programs. (And some of these are trivial, teaching a virtue a week by reading about it for ten minutes a day.) In true character development programs, either specific virtues are cultivated or the ability to control impulses and gain empathy is developed.[26] Providing all schools with such programs should be a high educational priority.

The ways students experience schools and the narratives they are told in story and play are more important for character formation than are lectures on ethics or civics. Experiences simply stay longer with young people and affect them more deeply than do words. How schools conduct sports is particularly relevant. We have known since the days of the ancient Greeks that sports form character. It is here that people first learn to control impulses, mobilize for the task at hand, work with teammates, abide by rules, and respect referees. In some schools, sports in effect teach youngsters that winning is the only thing that matters; in others, that it matters more how you play the game than whether you win or lose. We need more of the second kind; actually, we need none of the first.

A good society requires good people. It cannot allow character education to be driven out by parents and educators who are keen to prepare kids for college starting at a very tender age and focusing almost exclusively on academics.

To ensure that this core educational principle is heeded, an annual assessment should be made of all schools for the educational (as distinct from teaching) messages they impart and for their character formation methodology. If these are defective, schools should be encouraged to bring the experiences they engender in line with their desired educational message. Hard work should be well rewarded, minor infractions of discipline should be viewed as educational opportunities rather than ignored, peer mentors should patrol the corridors and playgrounds and cafeterias to help mediate verbal conflicts before they turn into violent fights, and so on.

Education that calls on young people to "Just Say No" (to drugs, alcohol, sex, smoking, and aggressive expressions) will be much less successful than education that provides positive and meaningful challenges, something to which they can say yes. All forms of antisocial behavior are low in communities in which there are strong positive values.

Educational, family, and welfare policies are often developed in isolation from one another and above all from work practices. But if people are to be treated as ends in themselves, they cannot be viewed as fragments–as merely students or parents or workers. Rather, they must be approached as a whole. Such an approach, in turn, requires a much better dovetailing of various public policies. One key example: School days end before many millions of parents are back home. No wonder a high level of juvenile crime occurs between 3 and 6 P.M. This gap needs to be bridged one way or another.

Voluntary Moral Culture Versus Censorship

Civil libertarians (and to a lesser extent, many other individualists) hold that freedom of speech is the most absolute of all our rights and should almost never be curbed. They hold that free speech can be limited only if it can be shown, under strict scrutiny, that such limitation is justified.[27] Hence, limitations on this right–for example, through bans on pornography and violence in media–are strongly opposed by many liberals (but not by numerous feminists). Social conservatives, on the other hand, are willing to introduce censorship, especially when it comes to national security needs and to curbing what they consider immoral or indecent speech. They support legislation to prohibit the sale of pornography, to introduce bans on pornography in the media and on the Internet, and to equate pornography with drugs and therefore to prohibit possession. Theodore Baehr, a steering committee member of the Coalition on Revival (a conservative Christian sect), calls for a film code that would impose a legal ban on "lustful kissing" and "dances that suggest or represent sexual actions." The film code declares, "No movie shall be produced that will lower the moral standards of those that see it."[28] Thomas Storck, writing in the *New Oxford Review,* a serious publication to which thoughtful Catholics and other social conservatives often contribute, makes "A Case for Censorship."[29] He points out that he favors more than simply censoring pornography; he would also cover the "expression of erroneous *ideas*."[30] More recently, Kevin Saunders, a law professor at the University of Oklahoma, claimed that states should "have the authority to ban completely the dissemination of excessively violent material."[31]

The communitarian paradigm advanced here, in line with its predisposition to build a largely moral rather than a statist order, draws on (a) a specific moral concept, (b) community-based rather than state-based mechanisms, and (c) a limited extension of the existing category of punishable speech. These are explored briefly next.

Right Versus Rightness

A communitarian way to deal with speech builds on a distinction between the legal right to speak and the moral rightness of what is spoken. While respecting the legal right of individuals to engage in obscene or inflammatory speech, a community is fully entitled, in fact called upon, to inform those who spout venom that it is deeply offended by their speech. Members of the community are well within their rights when they seek to dissociate themselves from people who speak in hateful ways.

Those who wonder whether such expression of disapproval by the community also has an effect should note the de-escalation of the rhetoric of talk-radio hosts after they were roundly criticized after the bombing in Oklahoma City. Similarly, although Time-Warner initially rebuffed William Bennett's public outcry about the foul rap songs issued by the media giant, it later fired the executives involved and sold that music division. It has been a long time since Jesse Jackson called New York "Hymietown." Even Louis Farrakhan has grown more circumspect. In short, community exhortations can go a long way toward encouraging members to express themselves in a civil manner and toward keeping most expressions of the mainstream media within some kind of bounds.

Urging the media to exercise some self-restraint is not a waste of time.[32] Although the media often protest at first, they then mind the community. This is evident in the way the media have by and large ceased glamorizing drug abuse, have increasingly depicted minorities and women in positions of power instead of as they had historically been depicted, and have reduced the amount of smoking and drinking shown.

Community Mechanisms

The community also has nongovernmental tools beyond the moral voice that enable it to discourage inappropriate forms of speech. The way the British press dealt with a gruesome legal case provides an example: In 1995, Britain had a trial that drew nearly as much attention in the United Kingdom as the O. J. Simpson murder trial did in the United States. Rosemary West was charged with the murders of several girls, including her own daughter, a crime similar to that of Jeffrey Dahmer. The British press, including the tabloids, agreed among themselves not to publish certain particularly disconcerting details of how the victims were murdered. Television stations agreed with one another not to show pictures of dismembered victims. They feared that such exposure would define deviance down—that is, would numb sensibilities, with the result that other deviant behavior would seem less so[33]–and vulgarize society. (This, too, is one reason why all civilized societies have stopped public hangings.[34])

Although American television has little hesitation in showing the gamut of gratuitous violence, by and large it refrains from showing frontal nudity (except on some late-night shows). Many television stations still beep some obscenities off the air. (However, footage of persons relieving themselves in bathrooms is a recent tasteless trend.) And most mainstream publications will not carry an openly hateful article or even an op-ed that is deeply offensive–for example, one that argues that African Americans are inferior or denies the Holocaust. In Congress, a member who engages in speech that is offensive to another member is under pressure to apologize, which puts some limits on what is said.

Those who fear that increased reliance on these informal social mechanisms to curb hate speech or indecent language would be tantamount to censorship should note the difference between limitations on expression that have been coerced by the government and limitations that the various media voluntarily agreed to follow. First, one recognizes that a particular television station or journal does not have an obligation to air or publish any particular speech. Second, unlike government controls, which tend to be fairly all-encompassing, informal controls always have exceptions. These allow the *Village Voice, Penthouse,* or even *Soldier of Fortune* to provide a voice for those who feel strongly that they must cross the lines set by the community for appropriate speech and for those who seek to hear them. Informal mechanisms ensure that even speech that has no redeeming merit will find some outlets while most of us are spared exposure to such speech. Still, much is gained when this kind of speech is treated as tolerable but not respectable or even acceptable, as opposed to when it is accepted as a regular part of daily expression. Some protection for children can be provided by parents and educators. For instance, parents can use technology screens, such as software that prevents children from accessing violent and vile material on the Internet. Some screens block access to a specific list of web sites parents find inappropriate; others block sites that have certain words in their web site address, such as "bestiality." The best filters limit access to an approved list of sites, saving parents the chore of doing so. As demand for these filters grows, parents will be able to download such lists from their churches and schools, among others. For an example, see a web site operated by Nell Minow at http://www.moviemom.com. Such filters should also be introduced in school computers and in sections set aside for children in libraries.

A Limited Role for Government

When civil libertarians are challenged on the grounds that a category of punishable speech already exists (one may not shout "fire!" in a crowded theater), and it is additionally suggested that this category might be somewhat expanded, the civil libertarians' first line of defense is the argument that even though there are victims of free speech, this is a "necessary price we pay for a free society."

What is the underlying logic that explains existing exceptions to the First Amendment and defines a line between the exceptions and all other speech? This line is particularly important because libertarians are concerned that even if it were justifiable to punish some speech because of its effects, it would still not be acceptable because banning some speech would soon lead to banning much more. (This is often referred to as the danger of a slippery slope.)[35]

The answer is that falsely shouting "fire!" is a form of speech too closely associated with action directly endangering lives to be allowed. Note, though, that this correlation is based on a probability and not a certainty. Nobody claims that every time a person shouts "fire!" it will cause some people to be trampled in a mad rush to escape. There is only a presumption of a relatively high probability.

A few other forms of speech that are now tolerated actually fall into this category and hence might be prohibited. A case in point is statements like those of G. Gordon Liddy, who informed his audience of how best to shoot federal agents, saying, "Go for a head shot [because] they're going to be wearing bulletproof vests."[36] Such speech does "qualify" for banning on the grounds that it facilitates murder. Drawing on the same criterion of proximity, one would ban meetings to exchange tips on how to seduce young children, such as those of the North American Man-Boy Love Association (NAMBLA). However, such bans should not be a major tool in protecting the moral order.

In short, a community must not simply yield to all claims of free speech; ways can be found to limit hate, violence, and vile expressions without introducing censorship.

Four

A Lean but Active Government

Government Essentials

ALTHOUGH THE STATE CAN AND SHOULD BE SLIMMED down, there are a number of tasks that must remain within its domain. During the administrations of Ronald Reagan, George Bush, and Bill Clinton, the market was given ever more rein and public controls were scaled back. Now there are some signs that the market has overreached itself and to some extent needs to be curbed. Two telling and major cases in point are health care and privacy.

Over the 1990s, the United States moved toward relying more and more on health maintenance organizations (HMOs)–profit-making corporations–to manage health care, reducing the relative role of the not-for-profits and the government. For a while, HMOs slowed the rise of health care costs, while providing high salaries to their executives and fabulous returns to their shareholders. But polls showed and legislatures discovered that the overwhelming majority of the public found this form of managed health care rather troubling. As a result, both major political parties are now moving toward limiting what HMOs can do to patients by introducing new government regulations, many of which have been grouped together and referred to as the patients' bill of rights.

Also in the late 1990s, privacy has become ever more endangered and has turned into one of the public's hottest concerns. Most infringements on privacy were made not by the traditional enemy of privacy, Big Brother, but by Big Bucks–select profit-making companies. Ergo, Democrats and Republicans on the national and state levels recently moved toward introducing new government regulations protecting medical, financial, and some other forms of privacy.

To avoid "ad-hocracy," we should draw on a systematic scheme that defines the proper roles of the government, so that as we correct the course changes of the 1990s, which have led to a sometimes invasive market, we do not overcorrect in the opposite direction and return to Big Government. Such a scheme follows, in which the governmental roles are briefly discussed. These roles are familiar, but in each we find a new, centrist twist.

Public Safety: More Accountability for Private Forces

A high level of public safety is a minimal condition for a good society. It cannot be stated often enough: Nothing takes us further away from being treated as ends than being subjected to violent crime. The end of a gun is about as far as one can get from being treated as a full person.

The main responsibility for public safety should be returned to the state. In recent years, American society has vastly increased its reliance on private policing (e.g., hired guards); indeed, there are now more than twice as many private guards as there are police patrol officers. (In 1998 the number of private guards was 1,026,723, while the number of police patrol officers was 445,632.)[1] There also has been a substantial increase in profit-making prisons and correctional institutions. Between 1990 and 1996, the number of adults in the private prison population increased by 5.6 times; by comparison, the prison population as a whole increased by 1.5 times during the same period.[2]

Experience with the privatization of public safety suggests that we now need stronger state regulations and closer scrutiny of privately run prisons. To enhance profits, private prisons have been hiring underqualified prison guards, using unsafe methods to transport prisoners, and allowing gross abuses of inmates. Indeed, some private facilities have already been repossessed by the government. For example, the Louisiana Department of Corrections assumed control of the privately run Jena Juvenile Correctional Center in Louisiana after guards were accused of depriving their charges of basic necessities, paying inmates to fight each other, raping inmates, dealing drugs, and laughing off teens' attempts to commit suicide.[3] One might wonder whether the severe problems encountered by the for-profit prisons reflected the particular culture of Louisiana or the nature of such corporations, being not well suited for this line of business. The fact is that privately managed prisons have run into difficulties in many other states, including Ohio, Texas, and New Mexico. If we continue to turn inmates over to profit-making prisons, we should subject those prisons to close monitoring by a new public authority or regulatory commission specially entrusted with this duty.

At the same time, communities should be allowed more opportunities to oversee the state's efforts to promote public safety. Incidents of police brutality, from Los Angeles to New York City, demonstrate that the police do not act vigorously enough to restrain their own.

Many cities still require civilian review boards to help ensure that the police do not brutalize citizens.

On a larger scale, on several occasions in recent years—as the market has been increasingly freed from public controls—market-driven considerations have been allowed to undermine national security. For instance, the conservative publication the *Weekly Standard* reported, under the title "Businessmen for Proliferation," that business lobbies blocked limitations on trade with China aimed at discouraging China from helping Pakistan develop long-range missiles capable of delivering nuclear warheads.[4] One reason national security secrets are so poorly kept in Los Alamos and elsewhere, according to the *Wall Street Journal,* is that U.S. contractors pressured the reduction of security because they found it expensive and burdensome to live by its requirements.[5]

There are other cases in which moneymaking was allowed to take priority over serious national security considerations in the age when the nation benefited from unfettering the market. Other examples include exporting top-of-the-line encryption software to other countries, whence it can easily find its way to rogue nations,[6] and the selling of advanced missile guidance systems to China. Moreover, U.S. corporations sold more than $15 billion worth of strategic equipment to China between 1988 and 1998; more than half of these exports were high-performance computers that can be used to design and test nuclear warheads and can simulate the performance of a missile from launch to impact. According to U.S. intelligence, China has utilized much of the equipment it bought from the United States to fuel military equipment exports to Iran, Iraq, India, and Pakistan.[7]

One urgent and major case, that of the United States Enrichment Corporation (USEC),[8] hardly requires extensive deliberations and provides a clear example of a situation that calls for reversing privatization. USEC's task is buying from Russia weapons-grade uranium that has been removed from missiles decommissioned under arms-control agreements with the United States. In this way, the United States seeks to prevent these bomb-making materials from being sold on the international markets. USEC's task is to convert the uranium into fuel for commercial reactors and to resell it afterwards. It works under the fine slogan "From megatons to megawatts." The corporation was privatized in 1998 and has run into trouble ever since. Although its executives and shareholders made out like bandits, the corporation continually runs back to Congress for bailouts. It recently scaled back its operations and fired a good part of its workers. It plans to close one of its major uranium-enrichment plants to reduce costs, despite pleas to the contrary by the government. The U.S. government is worried that USEC will undermine U.S. ability to meet its arms-control deal with Russia. Many legislators, led by Representative Ted Strickland (D.–Ohio), are calling for much tighter government scrutiny over USEC and are even considering demanding that the administration reacquire it.[9]

The specific cases are subject to considerable differences of opinion, but there are enough of them that the new administration would do well to conduct a systematic review of the matter. Such a review should lead to a strengthening of those public agencies whose job it is to examine and stop exports of weapons, special materials, and software that could seriously damage the security of the United States or its allies (e.g., Israel). Surely we can find ways to encourage the golden goose to keep laying her eggs, without stuffing her face with violations of national security.

More Certitude, Shorter Sentences

A major goal for the next decade should be significantly increasing the *certitude* (sometimes referred to as "celerity") that those who violate the law will be caught, those caught will be convicted, and those convicted will serve their terms. Such an increase in certitude will allow reduction of both the length of jail time and the harshness of the term (such as less solitary confinement and less reliance on high-security prisons), and at the same time it will *enhance* public safety. The result will be a more humane treatment of criminals and a greater chance of their rehabilitation, as well as significantly decreased public costs (after a transition period from the current system). All this is in line with our criteria for the good society.

This approach deserves some elaboration. People who are inclined to commit crimes are deterred by two factors that relate to one another as two variables in a mathematical formula: Size of penalty *(Pe)* multiplied by the probability of being caught and punished *(Pr)* equals public safety. A higher level of public safety can be achieved by increasing either variable. Given that *Pr* costs much less than *Pe* in human, social, and economic terms, increasing *Pr* is obviously preferable. Moreover, given that data show that increases in *Pr* are much more effective than increases in *Pe*, these facts alone provide a compelling reason for trying to increase *Pr* rather than *Pe* in coming years.[10]

This is not the current condition. Although over the last few years the probability that a person who committed a crime will be apprehended, convicted, and serve a sentence has increased in the United States, it is still quite low. Murderers are much more likely to serve a sentence than other criminals, but still, this holds true for only one out of two (47 percent).[11] For other criminals, for instance those who commit robbery, there is only a 1.7 percent chance that an offender will complete the journey from having committed a crime to serving time.[12]

Although these and other such figures can be contested (for instance, unreported murders are not reflected in them), the general picture that emerges is true: There is still room for considerable improvement in the probability that those who intend to commit a crime will be deterred by the likelihood that they will be punished by jail time rather than by further increasing the severity of the punishment.

True, some punishing of those who violate the law is an unavoidable feature of an orderly and just society. However, increased certitude combined with shorter sentences will provide the desired combination of ensuring punishment where it must be meted out yet curtailing the inhuman and costly handling of those incarcerated.

Given recent new evidence that several innocent people have been executed, the highly questionable effect of this extreme penalty on deterring criminals, and the fact that practically all civil societies have given it up, we should suspend the death penalty. A new study should be conducted to examine the claims in its favor, the ways it has been carried out, and how appeals have been handled. Such a moratorium is now supported not merely by liberals but also by Pat Robertson and some Republican governors, including Governor George Ryan of Illinois.[13] To make hanging people a political test of our elected officials' commitment to curbing crime or of their machismo is utterly incompatible with a drive toward a good society in which all people are treated as ends.

A Rich Basic Minimum for All

One of the core implications of treating every human being as an end is that all deserve a *rich basic minimum standard of living*, irrespective of their conduct.[14] Simply for being human, everyone deserves at least shelter, clothing, food, and elementary health care.[15] People who act in antisocial ways or do not discharge their social responsibilities—whether because of their parents, "The System," poor upbringing, or character failings–are not to be denied the elementary life necessities we provide to inmates, prisoners of war, and pets.

Providing a basic minimum will not kill the motivation to work for most people, as long as work is available and they are able. Though some will abuse the system, a good society should consider this a small price to pay for affirming the basic humanity of everyone. Throwing mental patients, alcoholics, mothers with small children, or anyone else onto the streets and cutting off their benefits is not compatible with treating all people as ends in themselves. For example, mental patients who are homeless need either to be provided with the kind of safe and healing community centers and family backup that were promised when they were deinstitutionalized, or they must be reinstitutionalized. Such a change in public policy is important both out of respect for their humanity and for the safe and orderly living of all other members of the community.

During the 1990s, welfare systems, which badly needed to be reformed, were restructured. However, here we see a clear case of overcorrection, arguably the most extreme of many that took place in the last years of the twentieth century. The reform entailed, in extreme cases, cutting off some people in toto: not lowering benefits but terminating them, and terminating not merely cash support but also housing allowances, food stamps, and Medicaid assistance for children. Over the coming years, these reforms need to be re-reformed if we are to cease the violation of this basic tenet of a good society. There is much room for deliberation concerning what exactly society owes each person and at what level benefits will cut into motivation to work and to refrain from antisocial behavior. For instance, furnishing cash would not necessarily be a part of such a state-provided (or even charity-provided) package.

Two colleagues who reviewed a draft of this text, and who generally are quite sympathetic to the approach followed in this book, were troubled by this last point. One feared that any return to welfare as an entitlement (or as a right) would open the door to a return to old liberal policies. The other was concerned that providing any welfare would undermine the motivation to work. However, these concerns seem best focused on the level and kind of benefits provided and on setting clear markers to prevent them from being unduly expanded, rather than challenging the basic tenet that certain minimums are due to people just because of their human worth and not because of anything they did or did not do.

Health Insurance for All

The majority of Americans, polls show, would rather not hand out cash to the poor but readily agree that they should be provided with food, clothing, and shelter. (How meager or expansive such provisions ought to be is less widely agreed upon.) Regrettably, the idea that everyone is entitled to basic health care has not yet been as widely endorsed.

Without maintaining good health, people are hindered from pursuing other parts of a meaningful life. A good society provides–either directly or indirectly via the state–everyone with basic health insurance. Politically it may initially not be feasible to provide extensive coverage. This invites critics to wail, for example, over the fact that mental health coverage equivalent to treatment for other illnesses is not included or that dental care is not sufficient. But attempts to start with a comprehensive program that covers all, as Hillary Clinton found out, may not be politically feasible. Such a program also deviates from the principle applied here. However, securing everyone a rich basic minimum of health care as a start should no longer be delayed if we seriously seek to move toward a good society.

What is entailed requires rather complex and extensive deliberations. Thus, it would at first seem that reimbursing patients for medication that saves lives would be at the top of the list, whereas reimbursement for drugs that merely ameliorate symptoms would be a lower priority. However, as anybody familiar with studies of pain knows, ameliorating severe pain is clearly needed if a sufferer is not to be deprived of most of what makes life meaningful. The dialogue as to what should be included in a rich basic minimum of health care may well start with ranking 688 different medical procedures according to their benefits and costs provided by the state of Oregon. It decided not to reimburse people for those treatments that rank higher than 568. Whether or not this is the right cutoff point is not something that can be determined without a detailed examination of the plan. It shows, however, that the discussion of what must be included can be made in specific terms.

On a more general level, health care is an area in which we must get the government more involved in controlling private-sector excesses. Some form of a patients' bill of rights may serve this purpose. Whether this is the best course is open to debate. But whatever course we take must be guided by the basic understanding that there is profound tension between treating people as ends and as a source of profit. Health care has always been a source of profit. However, in recent years the other half of the equation—serving patients—has suffered. The state must step in to ensure that a balance exists between making profit off sick people and treating them as fellow human beings—the way you would like to be treated yourself.

Public Health

The state is responsible for public health, which includes activities such as ensuring that water and food are free of cancer-causing agents, and preventing the spread of contagious diseases—in short, matters that are in the interests of the community above and beyond individual patients. In the near future, one of the best ways to reduce health costs will be to enhance preventive measures. Studies about the relative importance of changing one's lifestyle for health reasons, as compared to gaining more medical services, reach rather conflicting conclusions. (Moreover, liberals tend to stress the importance of changing the natural and social environment while conservatives emphasize changing unhealthy habits.) It takes little study, though, to realize that it is much more humane and cost-effective to prevent lung cancer by stopping smoking than to treat lung cancer, and to remove guns from the streets than to heal their victims. True, in other cases the connection between prevention and results is not as strong as in those just cited. Nevertheless, much could be achieved if we invested more in promising forms of prevention rather than focusing primarily on post hoc treatments.

Several studies across this field have indicated as much. For example, a past study of personal health practices and mortality found that good health practices may add as much as eleven years to the life span of a forty-five-year-old man; by contrast, a study of the effectiveness of curative services determined that they add only 3.5 to 4 years to one's life.[16]

Some illustrative examples follow:

- Public health authorities should be accorded the resources and administrative power they require in order to ensure that all pregnant women participate in prenatal care and that all children are immunized.
- Campaigns against smoking, especially aimed at young people, should be strengthened. Campaigns designed by young people themselves are especially effective and should be ex-

panded nationwide. It is legitimate to involve teenagers in seeking to ensure that cigarettes are not sold to minors and in helping peers to break the habit. Teenage antismoking groups such as TMVoice (Target Market Voice) in Minnesota and SWAT (Students Working Against Tobacco) in Florida have led noteworthy, influential campaigns; SWAT has been credited with helping to cause Florida's 54 percent decline in cigarette smoking among middle school students and its 24 percent drop in smoking among high school students between 1998 and 2000.[17]

- Voluntary testing for HIV among those at high risk should be strongly promoted, as should disclosures of positive test results to previous and prospective partners. This should be seen as a moral rather than a legal obligation.

- The Food and Drug Administration (FDA) should stop profit-making, corporate-controlled drug testing, which has all too often led to the approval of drugs that are either unsafe or ineffective. Among the drugs that have been recalled recently because of serious ill effects–including killing people–are Rezulin (for diabetes), Propulsid (heart medication), Duract (painkiller), Posicor (heart medication), Redux (diet pill), and Feldene (an anti-inflammatory drug). Drug testing should be conducted by not-for-profit centers, to be financed by the public and by fees charged to drug companies. Drug companies should be prevented from controlling these centers or making them dependent on corporate grants.

- The many billions of dollars that pharmaceutical companies spend on promoting drugs–some $14 billion in 1999, only a few billion less than what they are spending on research–

should be reduced, as many of the drug usages that are promoted are not needed or lead to reliance on drugs and are more expensive then those generically available. The needed drug information should be provided by facilities that serve both the health care professions and the public, by schools of public health or some new not-for-profit facilities.[18]

- Many injuries could be reduced and many lives as well as billions of dollars could be saved if, instead of investing more resources in driver education (which puts the onus on the individual and is not very effective), safer cars and roads were constructed. The same holds for tightening the conditions under which driver's licenses are renewed, better regulating truckers, and taking drunken drivers off the road.

- Domestic disarmament, a broad and encompassing form of gun control, has been demonstrated by repeated studies published by the American Medical Association to be a major way to save lives and prevent injuries at little public cost.

To reiterate: Illnesses and their resulting dependencies not only exact ever larger public expenditures, but they are also—on the face of it—incompatible with people's achieving their full potential. Massive new preventive care efforts are by far the best ways to reduce the cost of care and to foster fuller lives.

Environmental Protection

The environment is a quintessential concern of the common good. It does not belong to any one or even to all of us. It has been bequeathed to us to enjoy but also to guard well; to transmit to future generations in at least as good shape as we received it. To violate this stewardship is indirectly to treat not merely members of this generation but also future ones as objects rather than as ends.

It is high time for government to learn to show the same sensitivity to environmental concerns that it demands of others. The military especially needs to fall into line. To provide but one example: Cleaning up environmental damage inflicted by the nation's nuclear weapons program alone will cost between $168 billion and $212 billion. Although private corporations have spent many billions on preventing leakage from underground fuel tanks, state and local government agencies continue to operate thousands of such tanks, threatening the water supply of millions of people.[19]

Although considerable progress has been made in several matters concerning our stewardship of the environment, in others–for instance, the ground-level ozone buildup in our air; the numerous chemicals, such as arsenic, discharged from petroleum refineries that contaminate drinking water; and the high consumption of automobile fuel–much remains to be done. Simply to call for ever greater public expenditures for this important purpose or the imposition of more regulations on the private sector is not compatible with the centrist way. We have already learned that to some extent environmental protection can be reconciled with market interests and can even be a source of new jobs and technological developments.

In coming years, special attention should be paid to ways of expanding environmental protection at relatively little public cost by involving communities. The goal is to make a commitment to protecting the environment a part of everyone's sense of social moral responsibility. Most important, in the process we must further change our behavior, in ways ranging from recycling to bicycling.[20] These are hardly new ideas, but the lack of novelty does not make them less important for a good future.

Foster, Rather Than Undermine, Communities

To help sustain the three-way partnership, the government needs to do more to foster communities where they exist and to prime their development where they have failed. And it should take greater pains to ensure that it does not contribute to the ossification of communities by preempting their role. Hence, as a rule, the state should not be the first source of social services, especially not in well-off communities.

Small loans, child care, sick care, counseling, and much else is best provided first by members of a person's immediate and extended family, local and other communities, voluntary associations, workplaces, and faith-based groups. When the state must step in, it often achieves better results when it finances or collaborates with not-for-profit corporations and community groups (including faith-based ones) than if it provides the services itself–or pays profit-making entities to provide social services.[21]

To provide but one example: The worst mental hospitals are those run by the states. They are referred to as "snake pits" for good reasons. Bellevue and St. Elizabeth's, recently somewhat reformed, have long been notorious–although they are not necessarily the worst of the lot. Of the top ten psychiatric hospitals in the United States, only one is state run; the rest are nonprofit organizations. All ten of the nation's top universities are also nonprofit organizations.[22] It is widely known that, by most measures, primary, secondary, and vocational private schools are superior to public ones. But "private" in this context does not mean "for-profit." Nearly all private schools are not-for-profit; they are run by religious groups or boards of trustees. Similarly, practically all symphonies of any renown are not-for-profit. Thus, many of our best educational and cultural institutions are neither governmental nor market-driven.

Our efforts to improve government should include the formation of citizen-participation advisory boards for most federal and state agencies. Their task would be to find ways for citizens to volunteer, carrying some of the burdens currently shouldered by the state. These boards could also ensure that various agencies receive timely, focused, and informed feedback about their effects on the citizens they are supposed to serve. It has been fashionable to urge government agencies to treat citizens as consumers, as if the agencies were market-oriented. But treating citizens as citizens—as people who care about the work of the agencies whether or not they personally benefit—is more compatible with the communitarian approach than viewing them merely as clients.

All said and done, there is no cause for a return to an expansive Big Government agenda that swells public expenditures and generates massive new regulations. However, in the centrist way to a good society, the government has important roles to play well beyond the minimalist role of night watchman to which libertarian theory has relegated the state. Indeed, because over the last decades of the twentieth century the government role was excessively curtailed in several areas, a measure of reactivization—along the lines just discussed—is now called for.

Five

The Economy: Strong but Not Unfettered

A Principled Expansion of the Market

A GOOD SOCIETY ALLOWS CONSIDERABLE ELBOW ROOM for the market. It recognizes that *economic* well-being–the material wealth of society's members–requires that people relate to each other not only as intimate villagers but also as participants in a largely anonymous market. It allows for sufficient room for the instrumental relations required by a modern, thriving, and continually changing economy. Furthermore, it does not burden these relationships with regulations or social demands to the point that they hobble economic growth, productive work, or ample investment.

Recent experience in the West, and in countries in other parts of the world that have opened their economies more widely to market forces, lends strong additional support to the claim that great economic, social, and even human gains result from the freeing of market forces in countries that previously had greatly restrained them. This is true not merely for the command-and-control economies of the communist nations but also for paternalistic economies such as India's, and it even holds for much of Western Europe. However, it does not follow that market forces no longer need to be contained by some clear and principled set of boundaries that denote how far the market can be legitimately expanded.

Sustaining a Prosperous Economy

Squandering the Surplus Is Irresponsible

Keeping a budget surplus and using great parts of it to pare down the national debt will help to keep the cost of private capital low, hence encouraging investment and job development as well as keeping interest rates low for consumers. Any combination of large tax cuts and large new government expenditures, if they consume the surplus and introduce a new deficit (and increase the national debt again), should be considered irresponsible.

One can debate which of our political parties has promised more tax cuts, deductions, and credits, more new public programs and largesse. One thing, though, is clear: If budget responsibility is to be sustained over the coming years, the public will have to speak up on this matter loudly, clearly, and repeatedly.

Curtailing Corporate Welfare

An environment conducive to a sound economy encourages fair competition and ensures that public resources will not be used to advantage some economic players over others. Corporate welfare violates this principle: It consists of government handouts in the form of credits extended to some corporations or industries at below the market rate, special tax deductions, free R&D, exemptions from labor laws, and much else.

When the Clinton administration proposed curtailing the welfare system for the poor, liberals in the administration, especially Secretary of Labor Robert Reich, suggested limiting corporate welfare as a matter of social justice. The administration, keen to maintain its centrist status, reacted with horror to this liberal idea. But aside from its being unfair to cut the vulnerable members of the society off the dole while allowing huge corporations to feed from the public trough, one must note that corporate welfare is incompatible with a sound economic environment. It rewards those actors who are best at manipulating the government in their favor (often by providing campaign contributions to members of state and federal legislatures) rather than those who have proven themselves in the marketplace by better R&D, production, or marketing. Hence, in the near future new efforts should be made to review the numerous ways the government provides handouts to some private parties and to curtail these whenever politically feasible. It is a task the new secretary of the treasury and the President's Council of Economic Advisers should regard as one of their high priorities.

Investing in People

More for Schools, Less for Colleges

One can invest in education to make people better instruments or fuller human beings. Given that both investments are appropriate, the question arises how to best distribute the always scarce educational resources. Much has been made about the merit of investing in education and training as a way of keeping an economy strong, especially in the cyber age, in which the knowledge industry will continue to expand rapidly. The forthcoming biotech revolution will further increase the value of a labor force able to handle knowledge rather than objects.

And a good deal of attention has been accorded to investing in education at the higher end (in universities and colleges) as well as in training those most in need (such as the unemployed and welfare recipients). Although these efforts should continue, we ought now to accord higher priority to primary and secondary schools as well as to the absorption of immigrants if our endeavors to move toward a good society are not to suffer a serious setback.

Currently, American educational resources are incorrectly allocated. The American educational "system" is very top-heavy, compared to European and Japanese educational institutions (and to those in the United States before World War II). American primary and secondary schools leave too much of the responsibility for educating and training students to colleges. In many cases, American students' first two years of college are devoted largely to remedial learning. Japanese and many European high school graduates have about the same education that many of our youngsters have after two years of college.

And the United States sends roughly 60 percent of its high school graduates to college, compared to less than half of this percentage in many other industrial countries.[1] The result is an irrational, wasteful system in which hundreds of thousands of pupils who "graduate" each year are poorly trained and highly alienated from learning. They require later retraining at great expense. As a result, they are neither well trained to serve the postmodern economy nor prepared to be wholesome members of a good society.

Over the next decades, we should undertake *a massive increase in the proportion of new resources dedicated to the "lower" parts of the American educational structure as compared to "higher" ones.* Specifically, we need to slow down the expansion of colleges as much as is politically possible, while dedicating more resources to primary and secondary schools.[2] Such change in the allocation of resources is, of course, much easier (although far from easy!) when dealing with public universities and colleges rather than private ones. However, the latter also benefit from student loans, work-study funding, and many other programs drawing on public funds. These advantages should not be further extended until the other educational sectors catch up. The same holds for tax exemptions or credits now provided for higher education.

As teachers' salaries improve, schools will be able to attract teachers with more extensive preparation, such as those who now teach in junior colleges. And as the stigma of teaching secondary education is reduced (which should follow from better salaries and an increased influx of talent), American secondary schools will be able to carry out a higher proportion of the overall educational mission.

An especially high proportion of educational resources needs to be directed to primary schools, although both primary and secondary schools should benefit compared to colleges. The elementary reason for this reallocation is the much overlooked fact that to acquire skills and knowledge, pupils must first acquire certain personality traits. Recent reforms have focused on pumping more math, science, and foreign languages into students. But adding science teachers, labs, computers, and so on will achieve little if students are psychologically unable or unwilling to learn. Social science research shows that the required basic personality traits are developed early in life. These include the capacity to defer gratification and to control impulses.

Aside from being essential for making people members of a good society, these characteristics are essential for turning children into accomplished pupils. Focusing significantly more educational resources on early childhood development will thus be especially beneficial to the total educational effort. This will hold as long as early school years focus on developing character along the lines just indicated rather than on indoctrinating students with obsolete values or pumping the "three R's" into unformed personalities.[3]

For Now, First Priority to New Immigrants

Millions of immigrants, who are quite able to attend to their own needs and who command the skills and specialized knowledge to serve the economy and become full-fledged members of the community, are held back largely because of a poor command of English and a lack of understanding of basic American mores and laws. Hence new, additional resources invested in the education and training of immigrants will pay off much more rapidly and yield more than those investments in, say, people who have worked for many years in the old economy or those who have been on welfare for many years. This is the case because these people will need help in learning new skills and acquiring new bodies of knowledge that many immigrants already command.

This is not to suggest that these groups do not deserve our support. However, in recent years we have had large waves of legal and illegal immigrants. As the economy has boomed, the Immigration and Naturalization Service (INS) has responded to employers' pressures to look the other way and often to not enforce immigration laws.[4] Many states have very few INS agents anyway.[5] True, U.S. borders are better guarded than they were a decade or so ago, but they are still rather porous. And thousands of tourists with expired visas simply remain in the United States. If they are caught, which is rare, they can delay deportation for years through legal maneuvers. And when asked to attend a hearing, many simply do not show up.

As a result, there are currently an estimated 5.5 million to 6 million illegal immigrants in the United States, and their number is increasing by about 275,000 a year.[6] This is in addition to the 600,000 to 900,000 legal immigrants who enter the United States each year.

Waves of immigrants, mostly from non-English-speaking countries, have resulted in a significant increase in the number of Americans whose first language is not English. Their number grew from 9.7 million in 1980 to 15.4 million in 1990. About *half* of all public schools have sizable numbers of what are called limited-English-proficient students.[7] In numerous schools, instruction must be carried out in a large number of languages, including some rather esoteric tongues such as Vietnamese, Urdu, Somali, Hmong, and Laotian. True, it warms the cockles of one's heart to read about schools teaching in a score of languages in the same classroom, but teaching such classes is very taxing for the teachers. Although English-speaking students benefit from contact with a large number of classmates from distant places and cultures, anyone who has taught such classes—as I did—realizes that they also significantly slow the learning of native English speakers.[8]

Additionally, there is a substantial demand from adult immigrants to learn English and civics. Despite the fact that enrollment in such classes increased 105 percent during the 1990s, there are still long waiting lists.[9] Waiting time typically ranges from several months to years. In Los Angeles alone, some 50,000 people were on waiting lists, and the number would be higher if more immigrants knew that classes were available.[10]

Aside from keeping back immigrants, as well as the economy, the acculturation lag causes tensions in numerous communities that suddenly find themselves home to very large numbers of immigrants—often from a single country, such as Vietnam or Mexico. Many immigrants are not familiar with basic American laws and mores, such as traffic laws and those that ban spousal abuse and harsh disciplining of children. (One of the most widely shared observations made during the controversy over returning the child Elian Gonzalez to his father in Cuba was that many Cuban Americans in Miami were acting as if they lived in some other country, subject to a different law and culture. Critics quipped that Miami had been turned into a "banana republic.")

Another reason more investment in immigrants is especially called for is that if immigrants form ever larger communities of their own, their future absorption into the American economy and society will be that much more difficult. For all these reasons, investing in immigrants should be given high priority over the next years.

Last but not least, the cost of helping immigrants find their way into the American economy (and in the process, helping make it thrive as they prosper) can be kept down because much of the needed basic acculturation can be provided by volunteers, as long as corporations or communities provide the needed infrastructure of facilities (e.g., classrooms) and organizers. The program could follow, on a national level, a model drafted by Governor Gray Davis of California. In May 2000 he suggested making arrangements to ensure that immigrant children and their parents can benefit from voluntary tutoring during school vacations, after school, and on Saturdays. He aimed to include some 170,000 parents and some 625,000 children, all "new Californians."

All such endeavors must have the clear goal of providing the basic skills and understanding of American civics that most immigrants are clamoring for, while being careful not to suppress their subcultures. (A

1997 survey found that in Florida, 98 percent of Latinos felt that it was a necessity that their children read and write English "perfectly.")[11]

Unfortunately, immigrants' needs have been overshadowed by the debate over whether English should be made the official language of the United States. The right sees this as a sort of new loyalty test, while the left views such an idea as outright racism. Making English the official tongue of the nation is an empty and divisive symbol. What is called for is providing the millions who need it the language training that they keenly desire and that would largely benefit us all.

Sunset Regulations

To ensure that government regulations do not grow excessive and to keep the state from mushrooming, most regulations should be allowed to expire at preset intervals. That is, most regulations should remain in effect only if examinations show that they do not unnecessarily restrain the market, that they cannot be replaced by better regulations, and that there are no other ways of achieving the same purposes without regulations.

A More Accommodating Fed

Work helps build self-worth and is a vital foundation of ends-based relationships. Therefore, public policy should aim *not only to hold inflation at bay but also to stimulate the economy,* especially through low interest rates, which further increase growth and curtail unemployment. Recent evidence shows that much higher growth and lower unemployment can be achieved, without rekindling significant inflation, than had been previously assumed. This is especially important given how degrading unemployment is. In our society, more than jobs and income are at stake. Most people without work find it difficult to feel fully worthy or to be so treated by others. Therefore, public policy should place more emphasis on growth than on fighting inflation. An annual growth rate above 3 percent and an unemployment rate below 5 percent should not be considered levels endangering the economy's stability. (The economy has grown at a higher rate with lower levels of unemployment without causing serious inflation, and not only in the 1990s. The same was the case, for instance, during the Kennedy administration.) Thanks to the economy's increased flexibility since the development of the Internet, one can wait until the red-hot glare of inflation appears before dousing the economy with high interest rates.

Education and Retraining IRAs

Financial instruments similar to individual retirement accounts (IRAs), to which contributions might be matched by public funds for those with low incomes, should be made available for education and retraining. These would provide for retraining workers who have been laid off due to technical developments or unfettered competition from overseas, and would cover at least some relocating costs if necessary. Such IRAs would protect workers and benefit the economy by both increasing labor flexibility and improving the skills and knowledge of workers through lifelong learning and relearning.[12]

These and other such measures can keep the economy going strong over the next decades. Favoring them, though, does not mean that we should give the economy free rein.

Expanding yet Containing
the Economic Space

A good society does not favor a free or unfettered market. The market is akin to nuclear energy: It can generate an enormous and growing bounty of riches in products and services, but if the market is not properly contained, it may dehumanize people and wreak havoc on local communities, families, and social relations. Market-generated wealth can serve not only personal wants but also the common good, including culture and the arts, science and education, and public health and welfare. If excessively restricted, a good society cannot properly serve all these human and social ends. However, unfettered markets can be the source of undoing I-Thou relationships and allowing I-It ones to dominate. The main problem a centrist, communitarian approach faces is how much to increase the range for market forces versus where to place the containing walls preventing the market from overstepping its bounds. An obvious example is to uphold the ban on trade in human organs. Few acts more directly offend the treatment of people as ends in themselves, and not as parts to be used for someone else's purpose. We long ago outlawed trade in people and are properly alarmed when we learn about slavery in other countries. We should not treat trade in sex slaves any differently.

Many societies are currently making numerous incremental changes that lead to a grand expansion of the space given to market forces. These include greater flexibility in placement rules (e.g., those that concern moving workers from one job to another within the same workplace or from one location to another); lower severance pay; fewer vacation days; reductions in personal, capital gains, and corporate tax rates; less comprehensive health care and lower pension benefits; privatization of publicly held firms; extensive deregulation, enabling firms to issue tax-free shares to their workers; reforms of bankruptcy laws; and much else.

Many of these measures may well sustain economic prosperity and hence should be continued. Others threaten to breach the walls that should contain the market. As economic policies are typically discussed singly, there has been little discussion of the principles that ought to guide us in determining how much elbow room should be allowed for the economy to be further expanded, as well as where it should not be allowed to reach. Here are some principles that should guide us in these matters:

People should be able to assume that whatever changes occur in social policy, they will be left with safety nets protecting a rich basic minimum and that they will not be left in the street begging when they reach old age. People must be able to assume that even if various social safety nets are set at *lower* levels, by curtailing some benefits, no one will be allowed to fall through them.

Privatizing Social Security, or turning the administration of Medicare over to the tender mercy of HMOs, is incompatible with this principle. For the same reasons, stronger legislation is needed to protect pension funds from unscrupulous corporations that have misused their employees' money or systematically underfunded these plans.[13] Furthermore, stronger state inspections of workplaces and food safety are needed to ensure that existing as well as new regulations (e.g., concerning privacy protection) are adhered to. Many of these inspection systems have been thinned out in recent years, budgets have been curtailed, and regulations weakened. This trend should be reversed if we do not want our vibrant economy to break out of its retaining walls.

The details are subject to debate, *but in a good society people are accorded a basic sense of economic security.* This is increasingly needed as the market is given an ever freer rein and as social containing policies are retracted or loosened. Within the American context, this should mean that the following principles are closely adhered to in the future.

Work for All

In the year 2000, the United States achieved the lowest level of unemployment in thirty years, 3.9 percent.[14] However, economies that
rise also often decline. Hence, it is not too early to stipulate that to
the extent that one seeks to lay the foundations for a good society,
work ought to be available to all those who seek it and are able to
work. This is best achieved by keeping the economy growing at a
high level, as we succeeded in doing during the 1990s.

However, if there are no jobs in the private sector and the private
sector cannot be incentivized to provide them, then, as a last resort,
community jobs should be available for all those needing work. These
jobs may include making environmental improvements, serving as
teaching aides, or doing other work that would not be carried out if
it had to be paid for. Thus, community jobs will not compete with
other forms of job creation or with low-paying jobs.[15] Plans for providing jobs can differ in their details. However, to reiterate, given the
dehumanizing effects of prolonged unemployment, in a good society no one who seeks work should be left without work.

Freedom and Limits in Cyberspace

The notion that cyberspace is a new utopian world, where people
govern themselves and business need not be restricted, is without reality or justice. Cyberspace has turned from a virtual village into a
metropolis where people get mugged and need protection. One must
assume that as the proportion of the total number of transactions
conducted in cyberspace continues to increase, so will the need for
public oversight. Prescription drugs sold on the Internet cannot be
free from the protections that customers require in the offline world.
Taxes cannot be avoided. Messages transmitted by drug lords, pe-

dophiles, and terrorists cannot be exempt from the reach of the law. Libel on the Internet is not different from anywhere else. Young children must be protected from violent and vile materials.

Development in cyberspace illustrates a point often overlooked: Many laws and regulations serve to protect competition rather than to undermine it. Antitrust laws are an obvious example, favored even by such ultraconservatives as Judge Robert H. Bork.[16] The same holds for regulations that help "good corporate players" who are undercut by bad ones, including those who underbid them by selling defective parts, adulterating baby foods, evading taxes, and so on.

Curbing White-Collar Crime

White-collar and corporate crimes should be treated as seriously as are other nonviolent crimes, such as drug dealing. A number of corporations have knowingly marketed unsafe drugs, cheated the government out of large sums, or otherwise violated the law at great risk to the public. The fact that such offenses are often met with lenient punishment undermines people's trust in the government and fosters large-scale corruption.

The Art of Combinations

The tendency to view the state and the market as opposites, at least as alternative approaches to social issues, conceals the fact that some of the best and most important work of a society that aspires to be good is conducted either by the third sector or by hybrids. These are various amalgams in which elements of two or even three sectors are combined. Examples follow. Their purpose is to urge much greater attention to these neither private nor public nor communal bodies. Assuming that further examination of their qualities and limitations would show that in many areas these are superior to pure sector types, many more missions should be entrusted to these hybrids. Examples include:

- Religious institutions and voluntary associations, such as Catholic charities or Jewish groups, that provide social services but are financed in part by the government.
- Privately run or not-for-profit cultural institutions, such as universities, museums, and theaters, whose initial capital costs or start-up funds are provided by the state. These institutions may continue to rely on some partial government subsidies but should draw the majority of their operating funds from their gift shops, restaurants, entrance ticket sales, and so on.
- Vouchers paid for by the state to allow people to purchase community services or market products, such as housing allowances.
- Public corporations, such as the Public Broadcasting Corporation (which provides for public TV) and National Public Radio (NPR). These public media outlets are especially important in an age of increasingly commercial forms of communication. Pressures to commercialize them have already diluted their quality and ability to be of public service. Cutting public corporations off from annual appropriations, and providing them with a sizable endowment, would be a major step to ensure their independence from political and budgetary pressures.

Six

———

Saving the Rules
of the Game

———

CIVIL AND GOOD SOCIETIES SHARE ONE CONCERN: Conflicts that are unavoidable must be curbed by rules so they will not spin out of control or turn violent. These rules of the game, with which we are familiar from situations as disparate as football and debates on the floor of the Senate, can be applied to conflicts among different communities.

During the last decades of the twentieth century, especially during the 1990s, the rules of the political game have frayed. Both parties have engaged in ever more personal attacks on each other's leaders and driven several elected officials out of office. In the same decades, more and more politicians have been swept away from serving the public interest by floods of private funds. To rebuild a civil political system, to move toward a good society, two major reforms are required.

Decriminalizing Politics

When communitarians advocate finding common ground, they are often chastised by those who maintain that the essence of politics is clashes among diverse interest groups, that partisanship is the essence of democracy. (Some even argue that society is nothing but an arena in which various classes or races duke it out.) These critics scoff at what they deride as "consensus politics." They overlook the fact that conflicts, as well as political give-and-take, can take place without destroying common ground. Somewhat as married couples can, political adversaries can learn to stand up for their divergent interests and change their allocations of assets and responsibilities without being at each other's throats. Good couples learn to fight with one hand tied behind their back, so to speak. Similarly, communitarian politics favor respecting rules of engagement that limit but do not suppress conflict.

In several earlier eras and in recent years, American politics has broken out of this model, causing gridlock in Washington and worse: the criminalization of politics. The resulting climate of personal attacks, followed by vendettas, can be captured by the following anecdote told by Republican Congressman Tom Campbell (Calif.). He was walking down the Hill with several Democrats and Republicans after the GOP removed former Speaker of the House James Wright (D.–Tex.) from office following relatively minor ethics violations in the selling of his book. Campbell expressed some regret about this action and suggested, "We must stop doing this to each other." The Democrats responded, "By all means–immediately after we get your guy!"[1]

Some years later, Democratic Speaker of the House Dan Rostenkowski (Ill.) was driven out of office, as were GOP Speaker Newt Gingrich (Ga.) and GOP Representative Bob Livingston (La.), and of course President Clinton was impeached. A number of special prosecutors have been appointed who have charged numerous cabinet members of both political parties, as well as President Ronald Reagan, with all kinds of ethical and legal violations. Many of the accused were eventually exonerated, but only after incurring huge legal costs and irreparable damage to their reputations and to the trust the people put in elected officials. The politics of personal destruction is threatening to destroy politics itself.[2]

While the vicious cycle of personal attacks and counterattacks has subsided recently, it could easily escalate again on short notice. For instance, in May 2000 the Democrats brought a suit against House Majority Whip Tom DeLay (R.–Tex.) that charged him with extortion, racketeering, and money laundering.

To nurture communitarian politics, to contain conflicts, the representatives of both major parties need now to get together to work out a new, reinforced set of rules that curb political strife. This does *not* mean that if someone commits a serious offense the other side should let the offender get away with murder, so to speak. *It is necessary, however, to significantly raise the bar as to which kinds of transgressions should lead to attempts to drive elected officials out of office.* Indeed, in retrospect it seems evident that the kinds of transgressions committed by several of the elected officials mentioned here may have merited an informal or formal ethical reprimand or some other form of censure but not removal from office, overriding the electorate's choice. (This applies when the person has been directly elected; one can argue that in the case of speakers, the colleagues who chose them in the first place can remove them from this post. Still, the damage to the public trust and to the working of the political system stands.)

Nor does failure to adhere fully to all rules and regulations–such as those governing the use of publicly provided stamps or the places from which phone calls are made–justify years of investigations, public hearings, great expenditures of taxpayers' moneys, and the ensuing personal destruction. Both the public and party leaders must recall that under such close scrutiny, almost everybody could be subject to attack. There must be a better way of protecting the integrity of public office and maintaining respect for the law.

Most urgently, a bipartisan group of legal scholars and legislators should be convened to formulate new rules for dealing with the presidency. These new rules should be future-oriented; they should not aim to review past troubles, from Richard Nixon to Clinton, nor to exonerate anything former occupants of the White House did or are alleged to have done. Their purpose ought to be to prevent future damage to the democratic political system and to officeholders.

There follows a tentative list of examples of the kinds of issues that must be addressed. I cannot stress enough that their purpose is merely to show the kinds of issues that should be studied, not to conduct such a study here.

Partial Immunity for Acts Preceding Office, While in Office?

The question of whether or not a sitting president should be forced to stand trial while in office for acts allegedly committed before his or her election needs to be reexamined. The Supreme Court allowed a lower court to proceed with the case brought by Paula Jones against President Clinton on the presumption that such a trial would not hamper the president's ability to carry out his duties. The events that followed leave little doubt that this assumption was erroneous.

Thus, we must now revisit the question of whether or not a sitting president (and possibly other officeholders whose terms are limited) should be accorded any kind of immunity while serving. If the answer is in the affirmative, we should examine which allegations such immunity should encompass and under what conditions it could be revoked.

Views on this matter range to both extremes. Laurence Tribe argues that "the notion that the president would be like a king was implicitly rejected in our founding documents."[3] This position, which seems to reject any notion of immunity, disregards the fact that kings did not have set terms after which action against them could have been brought (assuming the clock on the statute of limitations would be frozen for those in office).

In contrast, Walter Dellinger argues in favor of an executive privilege for the president. He points out that "when [the United States] adopted the 25th Amendment governing Presidential disability, it was a recognition by Congress and the courts that the President's office was singular."[4] When Judiciary Committee chairman Emmanuel Celler proposed this amendment to Congress, Dellinger notes, Celler maintained that "the nation cannot permit the office of the President to be vacant even for a moment."[5] The implication is that the large-scale distraction caused by a prolonged trial would amount to disabling the president.

Akhil Reed Amar writes that "admittedly, the Constitution does not create executive privilege in so many words. But it does create a system of federalism and separation of powers. As a matter of federalism, state and local prosecutors cannot be allowed to disrupt the proper performance of national executive functions."[6] He recommends the enactment by Congress of "an omnibus presidential privilege bill" to include

> rules for when (if ever) a sitting president can be sued in civil cases; providing for tolling of statutes of limitation in the event of temporary presidential immunity. . . . The statute should also reaffirm the histori-

cally sound and structurally sensible rule that a sitting president cannot be forced to stand trial against his will in an ordinary criminal court.[7]

A good place to start further examination of the matter is to assume, as so often is the case, that both extremes (which are also often highly partisan positions) are unsatisfactory. Allowing any and all civil cases regarding actions of the president prior to election to proceed, disregarding how such cases hobble the president, seems untenable. At the same time, few would favor allowing the president to be completely immune from all infractions committed before his or her election, no matter how heinous the crime or however strong the evidence. Which intermediary positions should guide us needs urgent attention before another case is brought up.

Limiting or Eliminating Special Prosecutors?

Congress originally passed the independent counsel statute in 1978 as part of the Ethics in Government Act, which grew out of a response to President Nixon's firing of Special Prosecutor Archibald Cox. The statute was designed to free future investigations from interference by the president. The law set up a special panel of three appeals court judges who may appoint a special prosecutor at the request of the attorney general, and the new law gave the attorney general alone the power to fire a prosecutor.

President George Bush allowed the Independent Counsel Act to expire during his term as demands were made to launch an investigation into "Iraq-gate" allegations that the U.S. government had helped Saddam Hussein build his war machine. (Bush had already had to deal with special prosecutors during the Iran-Contra affair.)

President Clinton resurrected the law on 30 June 1994. Five weeks later, Kenneth Starr was appointed.

Since then, independent counsels have come under much attack for being unsupervised, taking too long, costing too much, allowing partisan politics to interfere with investigations, and undermining the political system. The process of appointing an independent counsel starts when there is some kind of evidence that a violation *may* have occurred. It may well be impossible to fully specify how strong such evidence needs to be before action is expected to be taken, but perhaps it can be made at least a bit clearer than it is now, thus somewhat scaling back the charges and recriminations that have been made around this issue. Furthermore, in recent years independent counsels have had a very broad license, allowing them to examine a large variety of events and documents. It might well serve the nation to limit those investigations considerably.

Because this law must be reauthorized approximately every five years to remain in effect, Congress has stepped in several times to try to correct some of its perceived problems by imposing some cost controls and by giving the attorney general more discretion to keep an investigation in-house rather than turning it over to an independent counsel. (In addition, Congress has changed the term "special prosecutor" to the current "independent counsel" to remove the implication that the officials targeted are criminals.)

But these changes in the law have done little to rein in the scope of investigations. Despite the criticism of previous investigations, the appeals court panel has continued to give independent counsels enormous latitude to follow whatever leads they come across. In appointing Starr, for example, the panel ruled that he could investigate almost any evidence of any crime that came out of his probe. Political pressures often make it difficult for an attorney general to refuse to appoint an independent counsel, or to decline to expand his or her jurisdiction, when it is claimed that such expansion is required to complete the investigation.

Congress did allow the independent counsel law to expire in mid-1999. Nonetheless, there have been continued demands for Reno to investigate Vice President Al Gore's alleged role in illegal campaign fund-raising by appointing an independent counsel. Republicans, notably Representative Dan Burton (R.–Ind.) and Senator Arlen Specter (R.–Pa.), have charged that Reno's decision not to appoint a special counsel on this matter was influenced by her political biases. Clearly, the controversy and charges of partisan politics surrounding independent counsels have not expired along with the statute.

To reform the way an independent counsel is chosen and operates, William Safire makes these suggestions:

1. Build some oversight into the way an attorney general selects outside, "special"–though not independent–counsels. An advisory board of judges appointed by all three branches could provide the names of outsiders capable of giving ethical cover to an administration under public pressure to show no conflict of interest.
2. Put more subpoena-power bite and professional investigators into judiciary committees to act as a whip on the backs of Justice Department investigators.
3. Make the currently ineffective Office of Public Integrity confirmable by the Senate.[8]

Surely there are other ways to proceed, but the need both to have some way of investigating specific allegations against serving presidents (and vice presidents) and to prevent them from turning into limitless expeditions and public spectacles is clear and present.

Clarifying the Meaning of "High Crimes and Misdemeanors"

Even if there are fewer charges that can be brought against a president and if the ways he or she can be investigated are curbed, the possibility that a president is found to have violated one law or another obviously cannot be ruled out. This leads to the question of how we should treat such violations. Few would argue either that any and all violations–speeding? jaywalking?–should lead to removal from office or that none should.

We obviously need a clearer and stricter definition of what constitutes "high crimes and misdemeanors." Abbe D. Lowell decries what he calls "the broadest and the least forgiving definition of the constitutional definition of high crimes and misdemeanors."[9] He suggests that the constitutional text refers only to those crimes that, in the words of George Mason, constituted "great and dangerous offenses to subvert the Constitution." Lowell also quotes Alexander Hamilton as stating that grounds for impeachment require there to be "injuries done immediately to the society itself."[10] Similarly, Representative Edward Hutchinson (R.–Mich.), a senior member of the Judiciary Committee under President Nixon, stated, when reviewing the conduct of President Nixon, that impeachable presidential offenses had to be "high in the sense that they were crimes directed against or having great impact upon the system of government itself."[11]

In contrast, Representative Lindsey Graham (R.–S.C.) argued (during the Clinton impeachment hearings) that the term "high crimes" might refer to "an important person hurt[ing] somebody of low means." Graham added that a high crime "doesn't even have to be a crime. It's just when you start using your office and you're acting in a way that hurts people."[12]

Further indicating how open-ended the clause is, Senator Robert Byrd (D.–W.Va.) quoted Gerald Ford on the matter as having said, in remarks to the House of Representatives in April 1970,

> The only honest answer is that an impeachable offense is whatever a majority of the House of Representatives considers [it] to be at a given moment in history; conviction results from whatever offense or offenses two-thirds–not just 60–of the other body considers to be sufficiently serious to require removal of the accused from office.[13]

Byrd attempted to narrow the definition: "even though the debates and actions at the Philadelphia Convention regarding impeachment appear on the record to have been comparatively sparse," to him the term refers to "corruption, maladministration, gross and wanton neglect of duty, misuse of official power, and other violations of the public trust by officeholders."[14]

Many other intermediary positions have been articulated. The need to narrow, at least to some extent, the possible interpretations of the clause before another case arises seems evident. We have learned from recent and previous experience that the bar should be set high, because overriding the electorate's choice severely strains the democratic process. It is sufficient to imagine how much our democracy would be undermined if a president from one party were to be driven out of office, following protracted and partisan impeachment hearings, and then the next president from the opposite party were to be subjected to the same process.

Recent deliberations have led to suggestions that there might be room for Congress to express its disapproval of the ways a sitting president conducts him- or herself short of driving the president out of office. Proposed measures that could be taken by Congress include issuing a formal censure of the president that would condemn wrongful acts but would carry no sanctions; drafting a "findings of fact" resolution that details the president's wrongful conduct but lacks the force of impeachment articles to remove him or her from office; and even obligating the president to reimburse the government for all or a portion of the estimated cost of an independent counsel's investigation into alleged misdeeds.[15]

At the same time, the bar cannot be set so high that it undermines the profound understanding that no one is above the law when it comes to serious offenses. We may well never completely define these offenses, but narrowing the definition is essential if the politics of mutual destruction is to be curbed.

Change the Succession in Office Act?

Currently, if the speaker of the House hails from a different party than the president (and vice president), the speaker's party may have a strong incentive to remove the president and the vice president from office, given that the speaker is third in line of succession. I am not suggesting that the opposition would drum up false charges merely to try to reverse the outcomes of a presidential election in this manner. However, when charges have already been brought up for some other reason, the institutional setup favors pushing them harder than might otherwise be the case, given that the presidency might be in play. How this act might be modified to remove such an incentive deserves much consideration. One possibility is to make the secretary of state third in line, secretary of the treasury fourth, and the speaker fifth.

Unblocking Presidential Appointments, Delayed en Masse for Long Stretches

The system by which candidates are confirmed by the Senate for judgeships and positions in the administration must be modified. Currently, any one senator can hold up numerous nominations literally for years. Their reasons may vary from personal pique to an attempt to extract approval from the administration for measures unrelated to the candidates. The number of such delays in recent years has been so large that an independent study by the Presidential Appointee Initiative (a project carried out by the Brookings Institution and funded by the Pew Foundation) established that those delays damage the government and the judiciary. It determined that during the Clinton administration, the nomination and confirmation process took longer than six months for 44 percent of all appointees. In contrast, between 1964 and 1984, the process took this long for only 5 percent of all appointees.[16]

Although such large-scale and extended delays in confirming judges and officials do not "criminalize" anybody, they constitute one of the forms that excessive partisanship has taken in recent years. And such delays significantly hobble the president's ability to do the job, poison the political climate, and undermine the efficacy, legitimacy, and prestige of the political system.

To make the appointment process less partisan, confrontational, and political, it has been suggested that senators who place a nomination on hold should be required to publicly air their concerns. Too often, one Clinton appointee told the Presidential Appointee Initiative, "the major holdup is often that a member of the Senate or members of the Senate oppose the nomination, but it's very difficult to determine who is opposing the nomination and for what reason."[17] Paul C. Light, the head of the Presidential Appointee Initiative, has asserted that there are now too many positions subject to presidential appointment. He believes that cutting the number of presidential appointees roughly in half "could be just the bargaining chip needed to win a streamlined Senate confirmation process."[18] Additionally, in "Obstacle Course," its 1996 report sponsored by the Century Foundation, the Task Force on Presidential Appointments suggested that the length of time a senator can place an appointee on hold be limited to a week or ten days; that a minimum number of senators must request a hold before one takes effect; and that any member of the Senate be allowed to offer a privileged resolution on the Senate floor whereby a vote of a simple majority of those present and voting could end a hold.[19] Such changes in rules may not be sufficient. Still other ways to preserve the right of the Senate to advise and consent, while preventing it from excessive partisanship, must be found in short order.

Executive Privileges for White House Staff?

It is difficult to imagine that future presidents will be able to perform their job well if they fear that any staff member could be forced to publicly disclose the contents of their private deliberations. This potential impediment to presidential action may be removed by according a given number of White House staff members a comprehensive executive privilege.

In her ruling on this matter during the grand jury proceedings against President Clinton, U.S. District Court Chief Judge Norma Holloway Johnson articulated a rather limited definition of executive privilege. She held that executive privilege should be used to keep presidential confidants from testifying only when their testimony would reveal "national security or diplomatic secrets" or confidential deliberative communications about official governmental matters.[20] She thereby withheld the privilege from those asked to testify about any other parts of the president's official business.

The effect of this and other such rulings has been devastating. White House staff members, it has been reported, often refrain from taking notes, writing memos, and so on because they fear future disclosure of these materials. The number of people attending meetings in which sensitive matters are explored has been limited. The net effect is to engender a climate in which proper work cannot be effectively conducted at the highest level of government.

One way to proceed might be to grant executive privilege that would allow a significant number of White House staffers (i.e., more than a handful but not all) to refuse to testify on any deliberations or documents unless there were compelling prior evidence that such materials pertained to a serious offense. There surely are other possible ways to proceed. But clearly, if stronger executive privileges are not extended to key White House staffers, investigations will tend to be unnecessarily invasive, and the work of the presidency will be severely damaged.

In Conclusion

One may disagree with any and even all of the revisions of rules of the game listed here yet still see the merit of shoring up the boundaries that keep partisan conflicts from turning into all-out slugfests.

Paul E. Begala, who served as a counselor to President Clinton, put it very well when he criticized his fellow Democrats for filing charges against House Majority Whip Tom DeLay. Begala wrote,

> The Congressional Democrats' racketeering lawsuit against Tom De-Lay . . . is wrong ethically, legally, and politically. . . . [It] represents everything I hated about the politics of personal destruction as it was waged against President Clinton. . . . It is wrong to treat the legal system as nothing more than politics by other means. In a free society, political differences are most legitimately resolved by voters, not courts.[21]

Once revised rules are provided for the conduct of the president, the same restructuring might be achieved for other elected offices, beginning with Congress. Reforming the rules and the culture go hand in hand: The more new rules are agreed upon, the less destructive politics becomes; the less destructive it becomes, the easier it is to formulate new beneficial rules.

For the same basic reasons, participants in conflicts within the society at large should abide by rules of civility rather than demonize opponents. We should move from what Deborah Tannen has called "the argument culture"[22] to a culture in which differences are openly discussed, while the disputants take care not to turn them into culture wars. The recent subsiding of identity politics and the renewed quest for common ground among races and between genders show that this communitarian line of thinking has considerable realism and presence.[23]

Cleaning Up Politics: Beyond Incrementalism

Few if any issues concerning the proper balance between the market and the state are more important than preventing a great amount of economic power from being converted into concentrated political power. A profound precept of a truly democratic society is that all members are equal citizens, regardless of differences in their wealth and social position. This precept is increasingly violated as the United States drifts toward a plutocracy. "One *dollar,* one vote" characterizes our current system much more accurately than the democratic principle of "one person, one vote." While it is true that candidates with wealthy backers do not always defeat poorer ones, all too often this is the case. Furthermore, an increasing part of the legislation enacted by Congress and state legislators goes to the highest bidder.[24]

Apologists for the current system argue that money only buys access, not influence. But in a democracy, access should be based on how many voters an advocate or issue has lined up, the potency of the case, and service done for the country—not the size of one's bank account. And access leads to influence. Corporations, unions, banks, and real estate associations would have to be both stupid beyond belief and in violation of fiduciary duties to their shareholders or members if they rained millions on members of Congress without any expectation of significant payoff. Anyone who believes that interest groups that shell out millions get nothing in return for their campaign contributions to politicians may as well wait for the tooth fairy to solve our social problems. Better, such observers should find out to which committee members the dollars flow and on which committees particular interest groups rain funds. In short, the claim that money buys access but not influence is preposterous.

Others point out that lobbying is a constitutionally protected activity, meaning that citizens have a right to petition their elected officials about whatever specific causes or interests concern them, whether or not they are in the general "public" interest. A leading political scientist, James Q. Wilson, recently wrote an op-ed essay in the *Wall Street Journal,* entitled "Pork Is Kosher." Well, not for all. It is fully democratic for voters to lobby their elected officials by writing them, sending them petitions, or buttonholing them and bending their ear. But gaining influence by paying cash on the barrel is a form of lobbying that the Constitution hardly favors.

The notion that there is no way to stop the flow of private money into political hands may well be true. However, experiences in Britain and Canada show that although politicians cannot be made saintly, they can be made much less subject to private money than national, state, and local elected officials currently are in the United States. In Britain, election costs are much lower than in the United States because campaigns are basically limited to a few weeks.[25] Each candidate is allowed to spend a small, fixed amount. (The amount is determined by a complex formula, but it is on the order of 9,000 pounds, or about $15,000, a puny amount compared to the millions spent by most American candidates.) If a candidate exceeds the set limits, the election results are invalidated and the campaign manager may be punished by a jail sentence.[26] Candidates are entitled to mail one leaflet to each constituent free of charge, and the parties are granted some free television time.[27]

The U.S. Supreme Court did strike down some forms of campaign finance reforms in 1976. But some others may pass constitutional muster. If they too are struck down, the next step should entail a push for passage of a constitutional amendment that opens the door to campaign finance reforms and to public financing of election campaigns.

The argument that one should not waste taxpayers' money on elections stands only as long as the public does not find out how much it would save if politics were cleaned up. Closing a few of the special tax loopholes provided to the superrich or to corporations, canceling but a few of the special subsidies provided to special interests, or discontinuing loans to the rich under favorable terms for which the public pays—all of these would easily cover the total costs of the next election. Thus, if we could only kill the weapons systems that neither the Pentagon nor independent military experts favor—say, the purchase of additional Sea Wolf submarines (estimated cost of each: $3 billion) or one LHD-8 helicopter carrier (estimated cost: $1.5 billion)—we would already be able to pay the costs of the next presidential and congressional elections and have a nice pile of change left. (Election costs are estimated to be about $3 billion.)[28]

Incremental reforms in a situation as grave as the one we currently face in this area are not likely to do much good and will only further disenchant the public. Comprehensive reforms need to include banning all contributions by nonindividuals, outlawing contributions from overseas and from people not registered to vote in the district of the politician to whom they contribute, and limiting the size of contributions to a small amount, say $100 per person. Public funding should be provided to all candidates for general elections, and to those who have collected a given number of supportive signatures from across the area in which they are seeking to enter a primary. Some free time should be provided on all media based on a public franchise, such as TV and radio.

The Federal Election Commission should be governed by people appointed in similar ways and for similar terms as judges, to enhance their independence. The commission should also be given a sufficient budget and the authority to exact penalties, transforming it from a lapdog to a watchdog.

There is room for hammering out details, but without comprehensive campaign finance reforms, there is little hope for ensuring that the government will be able to heed the public interest and serve the common good, advancing the good society, rather than being captured by special interests with deep pockets.

Seven

From Many—One?

WELL-FORMED NATIONAL SOCIETIES ARE NOT COMPOSED
of millions of individuals but are constituted as communities of communities. These societies provide a framework within which diverse
social groups as well as various subcultures find shared bonds and
values. When this framework falls apart, we find communities at
each other's throats or even in vicious civil war, as we sadly see in
many parts of the world. (Arthur Schlesinger Jr. provides an alarming
picture of such a future for our society in his book *The Disuniting of
America*.)[1]

Our community of communities is particularly threatened in two
ways that ought to command more of our attention in the next
years: Our society has been growing more diverse by leaps and
bounds over recent decades as immigration has increased, and
Americans have become more aware of their social and cultural differences. Many on the left celebrate diversity because they see it as
ending white European hegemony in our society. Many on the right

call for "bleaching out" ethnic differences to ensure a united, homogenous America.

Another challenge to the community of communities emanates from the fact that economic and social inequality has long been rising. Some see a whole new divide caused by the new digital technologies, although others believe that the Internet will bridge these differences. It is time to ask how much inequality the community of communities can tolerate while still flourishing. If we are exceeding these limits, what centrist corrections are available to us?

Diversity Within Unity

As a multiethnic society, America has long debated the merit of unity versus pluralism, of national identity versus identity politics, of assimilation of immigrants into mainstream culture versus maintaining their national heritages. All of these choices are incompatible with a centrist, communitarian approach to a good society. Assimilation is unnecessarily homogenizing, forcing people to give up important parts of their selves; unbounded racial, ethnic, and cultural diversity is too conflict-prone for a society in which all are fully respected. The concept of a community of communities provides a third model.

The community of communities builds on the observation that loyalty to one's group, to its particular culture and heritage, is compatible with sustaining national unity as long as the society is perceived not as an arena of conflict but as a society that has some community-like features. (Some refer to a community of communities as an imagined community.) Members of such a society maintain layered loyalties. "Lower" commitments are to one's immediate community, often an ethnic group; "higher" ones are to the community of communities, to the nation as a whole. These include a commitment to a democratic way of life, to the Constitution and more generally to a government by law, and above all to treating others–not merely the members of one's group–as ends in themselves and not merely as instruments. Approached this way, one realizes that up to a point, *diversity can avoid being the opposite of unity and can exist within it.*

Moreover, sustaining a particular community of communities does not contradict the gradual development of still more encompassing communities, such as the European Union, a North American community including Canada and Mexico, or one day, a world community.

During the last decades of the twentieth century, the United States was racked by identity politics that in part has served to partially correct past injustices against women and minorities but that has also divided the nation along group lines. Other sharp divisions have appeared between the religious right and much of the rest of the country. One of the merits of the centrist, communitarian approach has been that it has combined efforts to expand the common ground and to cool intergroup rhetoric. Thus, communitarians helped call off the "war" between the genders, as Betty Friedan–who was one of the original endorsers of the communitarian platform–did in 1997.[2]

New flexibility in involving faith-based groups in the provision of welfare, health care, and other social services, and even allowing some forms of religious activities in public schools, have defused some of the tension between the religious right and the rest of society. The national guidelines on religious expression in public schools, first released by the U.S. Department of Education on the directive of President Clinton in August 1995, worked to this end. For example, in July 1996, these guidelines spurred the school board of St. Louis, Missouri, to implement a clearly defined, districtwide policy on school prayer. This policy helped allay the confusion–and litigation–that had previously plagued the role of religion in this school district.[3]

The tendency of blacks and whites not to dialogue openly about racial issues, highlighted by Andrew Hacker,[4] has to some degree been overcome. The main, albeit far from successful, effort in this direction has been made by President Clinton's Advisory Board on Race. And for the first time in U.S. history, a Jew has been nominated by a major political party for the post of vice president.

In the next years, intensified efforts are called for to balance the legitimate concerns and needs of various communities that constitute the American society on one hand and the need to shore up our society as a community of communities on the other. Prayers truly initiated by students might be allowed in public schools as long as sufficient arrangements are made for students who do not wish to participate to spend time in other organized activities. There are no compelling reasons to oppose the establishment of "after hours" religious clubs in the midst of numerous secular programs. Renewed efforts for honest dialogues among the races are particularly difficult and needed. None of these steps will cause the differences among various communities–many of which serve to enrich our culture and social life–to disappear. But they may go a long way toward reinforcing the framework that keeps American society together while it is being recast.[5]

Limiting Inequality

Society cannot long sustain its status as a community of communities if general increases in well-being, even including those that trickle down to the poorest segments of the society, keep increasing the economic distance between the elites and the common people. Fortunately, it seems that at least by some measures, economic inequality has not increased in the United States between 1996 and 2000.[6] And by several measures, the federal income tax has grown surprisingly progressive.[7] (The opposite must be said about payroll taxes.[8]) About a third of those who filed income tax returns in 2000 paid no taxes or even got a net refund from the Internal Revenue Service (IRS).[9] However, the level of inequality in income at the end of the twentieth century was substantially higher than it was in earlier periods. Between 1977 and 1999, the after-tax income of the top 1 percent of the U.S. population increased by 115 percent, whereas the after-tax income of the U.S. population's lowest fifth decreased by 9 percent.[10] There is little reason to expect that this trend will not continue.

We may debate what social justice calls for; however, there is little doubt about what community requires. If some members of a community are increasingly distanced from the standard of living of most other members, they will lose contact with the rest of the community. The more those in charge of private and public institutions lead lives of hyperaffluence–replete with gated communities and estates, chauffeured limousines, servants, and personal trainers–the less in touch they are with other community members. Such isolation not only frays social bonds and insulates privileged people from the moral cultures of the community, but it also blinds them to the realities of the lives of their fellow citizens. This, in turn, tends to cause them to favor unrealistic policies ("Let them eat cake") that backfire and undermine the trust of the members of the society in those who lead and in the institutions they head.

The argument has been made that for the state to provide equality of outcomes undermines the motivation to achieve and to work, stymies creativity and excellence, and is unfair to those who do apply themselves. It is also said that equality of outcomes will raise labor costs so high that society will be rendered uncompetitive in the new age of global competition. Equality of opportunity has been extolled as a substitute.[11] However, to ensure equality of opportunity some equality of outcome must be provided. As has often been pointed out, for all to have similar opportunities they must have similar starting points. These can be reached only if all are accorded certain basics. Special education efforts such as Head Start, created to bring children from disadvantaged backgrounds up to par, and training for workers released from obsolescent industries are examples of programs that provide some equality of results to make equality of opportunity possible.

Additional policies to further curb inequality can be made to work at both ends of the scale. Policies that ensure a rich basic minimum, already discussed, serve this goal by lifting those at the lower levels of the economic pyramid. Reference is often made to education and training programs that focus on those most in need of catching up. However, these work very slowly. Therefore, in the short run more effect will be achieved by raising the Earned Income Tax Credit and the minimum wage and by implementing new intercommunity sharing initiatives.

The poor will remain poor no matter how much they work as long as they own no assets. This is especially damaging because people who own assets, especially a place of residence (even if only an apartment), are most likely to buy into a society—to feel and be part of a community. By numerous measures, home owners are more involved in the life of their communities, and their children are less likely to drop out of school. Roughly one-third of Americans do not own their residence; 73 percent of whites do, compared to 47 percent of African Americans and Hispanics.

Various provisions allowing those with limited resources to get mortgages through federally chartered corporations like Fannie Mae, which helps finance mortgages for many lower-income people, have been helpful in increasing ownership. More needs to be done on this front, especially for those of little means.[12] This might be achieved by following the same model used in the Earned Income Tax Credit in the United States and the Working Families Tax Credit in the United Kingdom: providing people who earn below a defined income level with "earned interest on mortgages," effectively granting them two dollars for every dollar set aside to provide seed money for a mortgage. And sweat equity might be used as the future owners' contribution—for instance, if they work on their own housing sites. (Those who benefit from the houses that Habitat for Humanity builds are required to either make some kind of a financial contribution themselves or to help in the construction of their homes.) Far from being far-fetched, various ideas along these lines were offered by both Bush and Gore during the 2000 election campaign, as well as by various policy researchers.

Reducing hard-core unemployment by trying to bring jobs to poor neighborhoods (through "enterprise zones") or by training the long-unemployed in entrepreneurial skills is often expensive and slow and is frequently unsuccessful. The opposite approach, moving people from poor areas to places where jobs are, often encounters objections by the neighborhoods into which they are moved, as well as by those poor who feel more comfortable living in their home communities. A third approach should be tried much more extensively: providing ready transportation to and from places of employment.

Measures to cap the higher levels of wealth include progressive income taxes, some forms of inheritance tax, closing numerous loopholes in the tax codes, and ensuring that tax on capital is paid as it is on labor. Given that several of these inequality-curbing measures cannot be adopted on a significant scale if they seriously endanger the competitive state of a country, steps to introduce many of them should be undertaken jointly with other Organization for Economic Co-operation and Development (OECD) countries, or better yet, among all the nations that are our major competitors and trade partners.

One need not be a liberal–one can be a solid communitarian– and still be quite dismayed to learn that the IRS audits the poor (defined as those with incomes of less than $25,000 annually) more than the rich (defined as those with incomes of more than $100,000 annually). In 1999, the IRS audited 1.36 percent of poor taxpayers, compared to 1.15 percent of rich taxpayers. In 1988, the percentage for the rich was 11.41. In one decade, there was thus a decline of about 90 percent in auditing the rich.[13] This occurred because Congress did not authorize the funds needed, although the General Accounting Office found that the rich are more likely to evade taxes than are the poor. This change in audit patterns also reflects the concern of Republican members of Congress that the poor will abuse the Earned Income Tax Credit that the Clinton administration introduced. It should not take a decade to correct this imbalance.

Ultimately, this matter and many others will not be properly attended to until there is a basic change in the moral culture of the society and in the purposes that animate it. Without such a change, a major reallocation of wealth can be achieved only by force, which is incompatible with a democratic society and will cause a wealth flight and other damage to the economy. In contrast, history from early Christianity to Fabian socialism teaches us that people who share progressive values will be inclined to share some of their wealth voluntarily. A good society seeks to promote such values through a grand dialogue rather than by dictates.

To foster economic and social entrepreneurship, taxes on capital gains have to remain low enough that they do not damage the economic engines of innovation and change, as has happened in many European societies. At the same time, taxes should not put those who labor at a disadvantage compared to those who invest. If taxes are withheld at the source, they should be withheld from both workers and investors (although withholding at the source for investment requires broad-based international agreements in order to retard the flight of capital).

The share of tax revenues provided by corporations has steadily declined. Gradually, the balance between individual and corporate taxes should be restored to roughly what it was in the early 1960s, when the economy was growing at better than 6 percent a year and inflation was below 1.3 percent annually. In 1960, corporations paid 23.2 percent of the nation's total tax revenues; in 1979, this figure was 14.2 percent; by 1999, it had dropped to 10.1 percent.[14]

Tax deductions are a major way that the public is abused and the common good is neglected. Such deductions are attractive because they allow politicians to rain large favors on their favorite interest groups without any obvious costs to anyone. Actually, tax deductions are no different from other handouts but for this exception: They pamper the rich, do relatively little for the middle class, and do nothing for the poor and near poor. Curtailing most of them should be a high priority for any attempts to reform the ways we govern ourselves. Such a plan is not visionary; many such loopholes have been closed before, most recently in the 1986 Tax Reform Act.

Cyberspace should cease to be a tax-free zone, a position already supported by both Democratic and Republican governors. Aside from providing unfair competition to all brick-and-mortar businesses, the absence of such a tax generates pressure on communities to increase property and income taxes as they lose a major source of revenue as more and more commerce shifts to cyberspace. The suggestion that this part of the economy needs protecting, as a new sector that must be allowed to find its sea legs before it can carry the burden of taxation, is ludicrous. The new economy is thriving, despite some not surprising shake-outs and corrections. If any sector needs protection, it is the brick-and-mortar economy. However, I am not calling for some kind of "industrial policy." What needs protecting, though, is the ability to collect sufficient revenue to pay for those public purposes that make society a safer, more decent, and more humane place.

The Knowledge Society and the End of Scarcity

Much has been stated, correctly, about the importance of fostering a transition to a knowledge-based economy. Such a transformation places a high priority on investing in people (in education, training, and retraining) as well as in technology. It is wisely regarded as essential for keeping the economy growing, productive, and competitive. Such investing also allows us to reduce menial labor as well as to enhance the kind of work that is family-friendly (by increasing the ability to work at home) and compatible with the needs of the environment (by reducing commuting). *However, surprisingly little attention has been paid to an attribute of a knowledge-based economy that by itself greatly merits attention: its potential to reduce scarcity and enhance social justice!*

Knowledge differs greatly from the other resources that an industrial society has traditionally relied upon: capital goods, from steel to petrol. Information can be *shared and used* at the same time. If a factory uses a ton of steel, that steel is no longer available to any other user, giving rise to issues of allocation of resources and scarcity. Old textbooks place this issue at the core of economics. However, in the new economy, when a programmer puts a design on the Internet–whether it is for a better mousetrap, home, traffic pattern, or whatnot–millions can use it and the inventor still has the original. (Some minimal use of old-fashioned resources is involved–say the charges for connecting to the Internet while copying the design–and therefore there are some trivial costs.) Similarly, many thousands of people can download a piece of music, poetry, film, and so on without it being consumed. While of course there are many items on the Internet that are not and should not be shared in this way, for instance those involving intellectual property and patent rights, and others are paid for indirectly (e.g., by watching ads or giving up on some measure of privacy), a very large number of new "goods" are being distributed on the Internet freely.[15] To dramatize how unique this feature of the new economy is, one may think about what Moses considered a stunning miracle: a bush that burned but was not consumed.

The more people satisfy their wants by drawing on free knowledge and cultural goods–say, by reading downloaded books, playing chess on the Internet, or joining virtual self-help groups–the scarcer scarcity becomes and the smaller the I-It sector that society must tolerate. Scarcity will never end, any more than history will. However, the more people (once their basic material wants are sated) draw on knowledge sources widely understood (including culture), the more ends-based their relationships can become.

Last but not least, there is a profound connection between fostering a knowledge-based economy and enhancing social justice. Practically all earlier theories of social justice are based on the idea of taking large amounts of resources from those richly endowed and transferring them to the have-nots. This idea raises obvious political difficulties. In many forms it also requires curtailing liberty to advance equality. However, if those whose basic needs are sated can draw their satisfaction from nonscarce resources, the door will open to a whole new world in which those better off will be much less motivated to oppose significant transfers of material goods to those less endowed. And those who possess less will also be able to benefit from nonscarce resources, once the state or the community ensures that they have the basic skills and resources needed to access the new world of knowledge.

All this may seem far-fetched, visionary, an image of a utopian good society. But although such a world may well be far in our future, its harbingers are around us. And the more we foster a transition to a knowledge-based economy with access for all, the more we approximate a less scarcity-driven and potentially more just world.

Eight

———

The Next Grand
Dialogue: A New
Counterculture?
A Religious Revival?

———————————————

THE GREAT SUCCESS OF THE ECONOMY IN THE 1990S MADE
Americans pay more attention to the fact that there are numerous
moral and social questions of concern to the good society that capitalism has never aspired to answer and that the state should not promote. These include moral questions such as what we owe our
children, our parents, our friends, and our neighbors, as well as people from other communities, including those in faraway places. Most
important, we must address this question: What is the *ultimate pur-*
pose of our personal and collective endeavors? Is ever greater material
affluence our ultimate goal and source of meaning? When is enough
enough? What are we considering the good life? *Can a good society be*

built on ever increasing levels of affluence? Or should we strive to center it
around other values, those of mutuality and spirituality?

The journey to the good society can benefit greatly from the observation, supported by a great deal of social science data, that ever
increasing levels of material goods are not a reliable source of human
well-being or contentment—let alone the basis for a morally sound
society. To cite but a few studies of a large body of findings: Frank
M. Andrews and Stephen B. Withey found that the level of one's so-
cioeconomic status had meager effects on one's "sense of well-being"
and no significant effect on "satisfaction with life-as-a-whole."[1]
Jonathan L. Freedman discovered that levels of reported happiness
did not vary greatly among the members of different economic
classes, with the exception of the very poor, who tended to be less
happy than others.[2] David G. Myers reported that although per
capita disposable (after-tax) income in inflation-adjusted dollars almost exactly doubled between 1960 and 1990, 32 percent of Americans reported that they were "very happy" in 1993, almost the same
proportion as did in 1957 (35 percent). Although economic growth
slowed after the mid-1970s, Americans' reported happiness was re-
markably stable (nearly always between 30 and 35 percent) across
both high-growth and low-growth periods.[3]

These and other such data help us realize that the pursuit of well-
being through ever higher levels of consumption is Sisyphean. When
it comes to material goods, enough is never enough. This is not an argument in favor of a life of sackcloth and ashes, of poverty and self-
denial. The argument is that once basic material needs (what Abraham Maslow called "creature comforts") are well sated and securely
provided for, additional income does not add to happiness.[4] On the
contrary, hard evidence—not some hippie, touchy-feely, LSD-induced
hallucination—shows that profound contentment is found in nourishing ends-based relationships, in bonding with others, in community

building and public service, and in cultural and spiritual pursuits. Capitalism, the engine of affluence, has never aspired to address the whole person; typically it treats the person as *Homo economicus*. And of course, statist socialism subjugated rather than inspired. It is left to the evolving values and culture of centrist societies to fill the void.

Nobel laureate Robert Fogel showed that periods of great affluence are regularly followed by what he calls Great Awakenings and that we are due for one in the near future.[5] Although it is quite evident that there is a growing quest for purposes deeper than conspicuous consumption, the faculty needed to predict which specific form this yearning for spiritual fulfillment will take may well be not given to us. There are some who hold firmly that the form must be a religious one, because no other speaks to the most profound matters that trouble the human soul, nor do others provide sound moral guidance.[6] These observers find good support in numerous indicators that there was a considerable measure of religious revival in practically all forms of American religion over the last decades of the twentieth century.[7] The revival is said to be evident not merely in the number of people who participate in religious activities and the frequency of their participation in these activities, but also in the stronger, more involving, and stricter kinds of commitments many are making to religion. (Margaret Talbot argued effectively that conservative Christians, especially fundamentalists, constitute the true counterculture of our age; they know and live a life rich in fulfillment, not centered around consumer goods.)[8] Others see the spiritual revival as taking more secular forms, ranging from New Age cults to a growing interest in applied ethics.

Aside from making people more profoundly and truly content individuals, a major and broadly based upward shift on the Maslovian scale is a prerequisite for being able to better address some of the most tantalizing problems plaguing modern societies, whatever form such a shift may take. That is to reiterate, what is required before we can come into harmony with our environment, because these higher priorities put much less demand on scarce resources than do lower ones. And such a new set of priorities may well be the only conditions under which those who are well endowed would be willing to support serious reallocation of wealth and power, as their personal fortunes would no longer be based on amassing ever larger amounts of consumer goods.[9] In addition, transitioning to a knowledge-based economy would free millions of people (one hopes all of them, gradually) to relate to each other mainly as members of families and communities, thus laying the social foundations for a society in which ends-based relationships dominate while instrumental ones are well contained.

The upward shift in priorities, a return to a sort of moderate counterculture, a turn toward voluntary simplicity—these require a grand dialogue about our personal and shared goals. (A return to a counterculture is not a recommendation for more abuse of controlled substances, promiscuity, and self-indulgence—which is about the last thing America needs—but the realization that one can find profound contentment in reflection, friendships, love, sunsets, and walks on the beach rather than in the pursuit of ever more control over ever more goods.)[10] Intellectuals and the media can help launch such a dialogue and model the new forms of behavior. Public leaders can nurse the recognition of these values, by moderating consumption at public events and ceremonies, and by celebrating those whose achievements are compatible with a good society rather than with a merely affluent one. But ultimately, such a shift lies in changes in our hearts and minds, in our values and conduct—what Robert Bellah called the "habits of the heart."[11] We shall not travel far toward a good society unless such a dialogue is soon launched and advanced to a good, spiritually uplifting conclusion.

Notes

Introduction

1. For much additional thought about this subject, see E. J. Dionne Jr., *Why Americans Hate Politics* (Washington, D.C.: The Brookings Institution, 2000). See also Deborah Tannen, *The Argument Culture: Moving from Debate to Dialogue* (New York: Random House, 1998).

2. New communitarians are not to be confused with Asian communitarians, who tend to be authoritarian. See Amitai Etzioni, *The Spirit of Community* (New York: Touchstone, 1993); Amitai Etzioni, *The New Golden Rule* (New York: Basic Books, 1996); *The Responsive Communitarian Platform: Rights and Responsibilities* (Washington, D.C.: The Communitarian Network, 1991); The Communitarian Network website. Available at http://www.gwu.edu/~ccps/.

3. The term "centrist" has been run up the flagpole by Mark Penn. See Mark Penn, "The Decisive Center," *The New Democrat* 12, no. 2 (March/April 2000): 8–13.

4. David Blankenhorn et al., *A Call to Civil Society: Why Democracy Needs Moral Truth* (New York: Institute for American Values, 1998).

5. The change was spearheaded by the so-called New Democrats and significantly contributed to the election and reelection of President Clinton. For a detailed discussion of the New Democrats, see Kenneth S. Baer, *Reinventing Democrats* (Lawrence: University Press of Kansas, 2000).

6. Michael Lind and Sean Wilentz, "'60s Liberalism Triumphant," *Houston Chronicle*, 19 September 1999, 1.

7. Among the numerous books and articles written on the third way are the following: Tony Blair, *The Third Way: New Politics for the New Century* (London: Fabian Society, 1998); Al From, "The New Democrat Decade," *The New Democrat* 11, no. 6 (November/December 1999): 28; Al From, "Understanding the Third Way," *The New Democrat* 10, no. 5 (September/October 1998): 28; Anthony Giddens, *The*

Third Way (Cambridge: Polity Press, 1998); Fred Siegel and Will Marshall, "Liberalism's Lost Tradition," *The New Democrat* 7, no. 5 (September/October 1995): 8–13.

8. Quoted in E. J. Dionne Jr., "A Fourth Way," *Washington Post*, 30 March 1999, A17.

Chapter 1

1. Martin Buber, *I and Thou*, trans. Walter Kaufmann (New York: Simon and Schuster, 1970). Unlike other philosophers and bodies of ethics that focus on the way ego is to treat alter–for instance, "Do unto others as you wish others to do unto you"–Buber looks at the relationship as created by all parties jointly, which renders his ethics less ego centered.

Chapter 2

1. John Gray, *After Social Democracy* (London: Demos, 1996), 16. As Michael Sandel has also stated, thoroughly independent individualism "rules out the possibility of any attachment . . . able to reach beyond our values and sentiments to engage our identity itself." Michael Sandel, *Liberalism and the Limits of Justice*, 2nd ed. (New York: Cambridge University Press, 1998), 62. Robert Putman recently added much more evidence in support of this line of thinking in his book *Bowling Alone: The Collapse and Revival of American Community* (New York: Simon and Schuster, 2000).

2. The reason for this is that social services are labor intensive, and labor costs rise more rapidly than capital costs because labor flows are not nearly as fluid and global as capital flows. Ergo, workers in one country have a greater ability to gain or maintain higher wages and benefits than those in another country. In contrast, banks and other financial institutions cannot charge significantly higher interest rates than similar institutions in other countries. For instance, the differences in the yield that American and European banks provide are minuscule compared to the differences in salaries and benefits their workers earn.

3. Alan Ehrenhalt, *The Lost City: The Forgotten Virtues of Community in America* (New York: Basic Books, 1996).

4. Will Marshall, "The Rules of Reciprocity," *Blueprint* 3 (Spring 1999): 39.

5. Marc Freedman, *Prime Time: How Baby Boomers Will Revolutionize Retirement and Transform America* (New York: Public Affairs, 1999).

6. The National Health Service Corps, "Twenty-Five Years and Beyond." Available at http://www.bphc.hrsa.dhhs.gov/nhsc/Pages/25_beyond/beyond_

intro.htm. Accessed on 17 May 2000. Dolores Kong, "US Hopes to Revitalize National Health Service Corps," *Boston Globe*, 19 April 1993, 49.

7. For a compelling example, see the discussion of schools and community building by Thomas J. Sergiovanni in his *Building Community in Schools* (San Francisco: Jossey Bass, 1994). See also Daniel J. Brown, *Schools with Heart: Voluntarism and Public Education* (Boulder, Colo.: Westview Press, 1998); Carolyn Denham and Amitai Etzioni, *Community Schools* (Washington, D.C.: The Communitarian Network, 1997).

8. Harry C. Boyte, *Commonwealth: A Return to Citizen Politics* (New York: Free Press, 1989).

9. Amitai Etzioni and Oren Etzioni, "Face-to-Face and Computer-Mediated Communities: A Comparative Analysis," *The Information Society* 15, no. 4 (October/December 1999): 241–248.

10. Andrew Michael Cohill and Andrea Lee Kavanaugh, eds., *Community Networks: Lessons from Blacksburg Virginia* (Boston: Artech House Publishers, 1997).

11. Andres Duany, Elizabeth Plater-Zyberk, and Jeff Speck, *Suburban Nation: The Rise of Sprawl and the Decline of the American Dream* (New York: North Point Press, 2000).

12. "With Help from a Hidden Hand," *The Economist*, 12 February 2000, 28.

13. Joe Frolik, "Using Faith to Find Solutions to Poverty," *Indianapolis Plain Dealer*, 28 November 1999, 1A; Dan Coats, "When Redistribution and Economic Growth Fail," *The Responsive Community* 6, no. 1 (Winter 1995/1996): 4; Stephen Goldsmith, *The Twenty-First Century City: Resurrecting Urban America* (Washington, D.C.: Regnery Publishing, Inc., 1997).

14. "With Help from a Hidden Hand," 28.

15. Ibid.

16. Amy Sherman, *The Growing Impact of Charitable Choice: A Catalogue of New Collaborations Between Government and Faith-Based Organizations in Nine States* (Annapolis, Md.: The Center for Public Justice, March 2000).

17. For more discussion, see Brian Forst, "Police in the Community, Community in the Police," *The Responsive Community* 3, no. 3 (Summer 1993): 57–62.

18. Caroline G. Nicholl, *Community Policing, Community Justice, and Restorative Justice: Exploring the Links for the Delivery of a Balanced Approach to Public Safety* (Washington, D.C.: U.S. Department of Justice, Office of Community Oriented Policing Services, 1999).

19. See Amitai Etzioni, "Sex Offenders' Privacy Versus Children's Safety: Megan's Laws and the Alternatives," in his *The Limits of Privacy* (New York: Basic Books, 1999), 43–74.

20. Amitai Etzioni and David E. Carney, eds., *Repentance* (Lanham, Md.: Rowman and Littlefield Publishers, Inc., 1997).

21. Todd R. Clear and David R. Karp, *The Community Justice Ideal* (Boulder, Colo.: Westview Press, 1999).

Chapter 3

1. Robert Bellah, Richard Madsen, William M. Sullivan, Ann Swidler, and Steven M. Tipton, *Habits of the Heart: Individualism and Commitment in American Life* (Berkeley and Los Angeles: University of California Press, 1985).

2. Alan Wolfe, *One Nation, After All* (New York: Penguin, 1998), and "The Pursuit of Autonomy," *New York Times Magazine*, 7 May 2000, 53.

3. See, for instance, Robert Sampson, "Neighborhoods and Violent Crime: A Multilevel Study of Collective Efficacy," *Science* 277 (14 August 1997): 918–924.

4. Allen M. Fremont and Chloe E. Bird, "Integrating Sociological and Biological Models: An Editorial," *Journal of Health and Social Behavior* 40, no. 2 (June 1999): 126–129.

5. Jack Stuster, *Bold Endeavors: Lessons from Polar and Space Exploration* (Annapolis, Md.: Naval Institute Press, 1996), 8.

6. See Irwin Altman, "An Ecological Approach to the Functioning of Socially Isolated Groups," in John E. Rasmussen, ed., *Man in Isolation and Confinement* (Chicago: Aldine Publishing Co., 1973), 241–270; A. F. Barabaz, "Antarctic Isolation and Imaginative Involvement: Preliminary Findings," *International Journal of Clinical and Experimental Hypnosis* 32 (1984): 296–300; Robert Johnson, *Culture and Crisis in Confinement* (Lexington, Mass.: Lexington Books, 1976); Albert A. Harrison, Yvonne A. Clearwater, and Christopher P. McKay, *From Antarctica to Outer Space: Life in Isolation and Confinement* (New York: Springer-Verlag, 1991).

7. Leo Srole et al., *Mental Health in the Metropolis: The Midtown Manhattan Study* (New York: McGraw-Hill, 1962).

8. Millard Walz, *Social Isolation and Social Mediators of the Stress of Illness* (Hamburg, Germany: Lit Verlag, 1994), 56–57.

9. Laura Fratiglioni et al., "Influence of Social Network on Occurrence of Dementia," *The Lancet* 355, no. 9212 (15 April 2000): 1315.

10. Mary Lou Hurley and Lisa Schiff, "This Town Made Wellness a Way of Life," *Business and Health* 14, no. 12 (December 1996): 39–43.

11. Ibid.

12. Ibid.

13. Ibid.

14. Suzanne Goldsmith, *The Takoma Orange Hats: Fighting Drugs and Building Community in Washington, DC* (Washington, D.C.: The Communitarian Network, 1994).

15. Jeffrey S. Luke and Kathryn Robb Neville, "Curbing Teen Pregnancy: A Divided Community Acts Together," *The Responsive Community* 8, no. 3 (Summer 1998): 62–72.

16. Federal Bureau of Investigation, "Section 2, Table 16, Rate: Number of Crimes per 100,000 Inhabitants by Population Group," *Crime in the United States 1998: Uniform Crime Report* (Washington, D.C.: Government Printing Office, 1998), 188–189. Available at http://www.fbi.gov/ucr/98cius.htm. Accessed 14 August 2000.

17. Mary Ann Glendon, *Rights Talk: The Impoverishment of Political Discourse* (New York: Free Press, 1991).

18. Although I generally agree with Anthony Giddens, we differ on this point. He writes, "Government has a whole cluster of responsibilities for its citizens and others, including the protection of the vulnerable. Old-style democracy, however, was inclined to treat rights as unconditional claims. With expanding individualism should come an extension of individual obligations. . . . As an ethical principle, 'no rights without responsibilities' must apply not only to welfare recipients, but to everyone." Giddens, *The Third Way*, 65–66.

19. For more discussion, see Charles Moscos, *A Call to Civic Service* (New York: Twentieth Century Fund/Free Press, 1988).

20. "Inclusion refers in its broadest sense to citizenship, to the civil and political rights and obligations that all members of a society should have, not just formally, but as a reality of their lives." Giddens, *The Third Way*, 102–103.

21. Philip Selznick, "Social Justice: A Communitarian Perspective," manuscript, no date.

22. Philip Selznick, *The Moral Commonwealth: Social Theory and the Promise of Community* (Berkeley and Los Angeles: University of California Press, 1992).

23. Amitai Etzioni, "Medical Records: Big Brother Versus Big Bucks," in his *The Limits of Privacy* (New York: Basic Books, 1999), 139–182.

24. For further discussion of science courts, see Allan Mazur, "The Science Court: Reminiscence and Retrospective," *Risk* 1, no. 4 (1993): 161.

25. "National Reading Panel Report Due out Soon," *Reading Today* 17, no. 4 (February/March 2000): 6.

26. For the reasons for this position, see Amitai Etzioni, *The Spirit of Community* (New York: Crown Publishers, Inc., 1993), chapter 3.

27. Alexander Meiklejohn writes, "No one who reads with care the text of the First Amendment can fail to be startled by its absoluteness. The phrase, 'Congress shall make no law . . . abridging the freedom of speech,' is unqualified. It admits no exceptions. To say that no laws of any given type shall be made means that no laws of that type shall, under any circumstances, be made." Alexander Meiklejohn, *Free Speech and Its Relation to Self-Government* (Port Washington, N.Y.: Kennikat Press, 1972), 17.

28. Quoted in Robert Boston, *Why the Religious Right Is Wrong* (Buffalo, N.Y.: Prometheus Books, 1993), 189.

29. Thomas Storck, "A Case for Censorship," *New Oxford Review,* May 1996, 23.

30. Ibid.

31. Kevin Saunders, "Media Violence and the Obscenity Exception to the First Amendment," *William and Mary Bill of Rights Journal* 3 (Summer 1994): 107.

32. For example, Patrick Glynn's project "An Appeal to Hollywood," sponsored by the Institute for Communitarian Policy Studies, calls for a voluntary code of conduct for depictions of violence in the media; see the Institute for Communitarian Policy Studies web site at http://www.gwu.edu/~icps/.

33. Daniel Patrick Moynihan, "Defining Deviancy Down," *American Scholar* 62, no. 1 (1993): 17–30.

34. James A. MacCafferty, ed., *Capital Punishment* (New York: Aldine Atherton, 1972), 43; Walter Berns, *For Capital Punishment* (New York: Basic Books, 1979).

35. Douglas N. Walton, *Slippery Slope Arguments* (New York: Oxford University Press, 1992).

36. G. Gordon Liddy, *G. Gordon Liddy Show*, WJFK-FM, 26 August 1994.

Chapter 4

1. U.S. Bureau of Labor Statistics, "National Industry-Occupation Employment Matrix," 1999. Available at ftp://ftp.bls.gov/pub/special.requests/ep/IND-OCC.MatrixOcc_PDF/OCC0514.df and ftp://ftp.bls.gov/pub/special.requests/ep/IND OCC.Matrix/Occ_PDF/OCC0524.pdf. Accessed on 15 August 2000.

2. Charles Thomas, "Ten Year Growth in Rated Capacity of Private Secure Adult Correctional Facilities," *Private Adult Correctional Facility Census*. Avail-

able at http://web.crim.ufl.edu/pcp/census/1999/Figure1.html. Accessed on 14 August 2000. U.S. Bureau of Justice Statistics Correctional Surveys, "Correctional Populations in the United States 1996," 1999. Available at http://www.ojp.usdoj.gov/bjs/glance/corr2.txt. Accessed on 15 August 2000.

3. Steve Ritea, "Jena Jail Doomed from Start, Experts Say, Profit Motive Blamed for Poor Conditions," *New Orleans Times-Picayune*, 30 April 2000, A1; Fox Butterfield, "Company to Stop Operating Troubled Prison," *New York Times*, 27 April 2000, A21.

4. "Businessmen for Proliferation," *Weekly Standard*, 17 July 2000, 3.

5. Neil King Jr., "Case of Lost-and-Found Disk Drives Demonstrates Weakness of U.S. Systems for Protecting Secrets," *Wall Street Journal*, 5 July 2000, A24.

6. Amitai Etzioni, "Deciphering Encrypted Messages: A Prolonged Deadlock and an Unholy War," in his *The Limits of Privacy* (New York: Basic Books, 1999), 75–102.

7. Wisconsin Project on Nuclear Arms Control, *U.S. Exports to China, 1988–1998: Fueling Proliferation* (Washington, D.C.: The Wisconsin Project on Nuclear Arms Control, April 1999).

8. Technically, after privatization, the formerly public United States Enrichment Corporation became a subsidiary of USEC, a private company.

9. Representative Ted Strickland (D.–Ohio), statement before the House of Representatives, 5 November 1999, "Critics Question USEC's Request for $200 Million." Available at http://thomas.loc.gov/cgi-bin/query/D?r106:1:./temp/~r106BsCEEq::. Accessed on 10 May 2000. For press reports, see Jonathan Riskind, "Piketon Workers Wary of Government's Offer," *Columbus Dispatch*, 9 May 2000, 5A; James Carroll and James Malone, "Safety Data Erased at Uranium Plants, Records Show US Didn't Clear Firms' Actions," *Louisville (Kentucky) Courier Journal*, 30 April 2000, 1A.

10. Jeffrey Grogger, "Certainty Versus Severity of Punishment," *Economic Inquiry* 29 (April 1991): 297–309, especially page 304.

11. Patrick A. Langan and David P. Farrington, "Crime and Justice in the United States and in England and Wales, 1981–1996" (Washington, D.C.: Government Printing Office, October 1998).

12. Ibid.

13. Clarence Page, "Ranks of Death Penalty Critics Growing," *Houston Chronicle*, 18 April 2000, A18.

14. Stephen Nathanson, *Economic Justice* (New York: Prentice Hall Academic, 1998).

15. Ibid.

16. Nedra B. Belloc, "Relationship of Health Practices and Mortality," *Preventive Medicine* 2 (1973): 67. See also John P. Bunker, Howard S. Frazier, and Frederick Mosteller, "The Role of Medical Care in Determining Health: Creating an Inventory of Benefits," in Benjamin C. Amick, Sol Levine, Alvin R. Tarlov, Diana Chapman Walsh, eds., *Society and Health* (New York: Oxford University Press, 1995), 321.

17. Florida State Department of Health, Office of Tobacco Control, *2000 Florida Youth Tobacco Survey Results,* vol. 3, report 1 (Tallahassee, Fla.: Florida Department of Health, 2000); "Teens Are Heading Anti-Smoking Ads," editorial, *Tampa Tribune*, 25 March 2000, 2.

18. In advancing this policy proposal, I draw on the ideas of Raymond Woosley of the Georgetown University Medical Center. See Alastair J. J. Wood, Michael C. Stein, and Raymond Woosley, "Making Medicines Safer: The Need for an Independent Drug Safety Board," *The New England Journal of Medicine* 339, no. 25 (17 December 1998): 1851–1854.

19. Associated Press, "Cost Estimates Rise for Nuclear Cleanup," *New York Times*, 20 April 2000, A16.

20. For a discussion of environmentalism and the role that both federal and civic sectors should play, see John DeWitt, *Civic Environmentalism: Alternatives to Regulation in States and Communities* (Washington, D.C.: CQ Press, 1994). Another source explaining today's environmental issues is Mary K. Theodore and Louis Theodore, *Major Environmental Issues Facing the Twenty-First Century* (Upper Saddle River, N.J.: Prentice Hall, 1996). And for a very strongly pro-environmental book, see Al Gore, *Earth in the Balance: Ecology and the Human Spirit* (New York: Plume, 1993).

21. For additional discussion see Stephen Goldsmith, *The Twenty-first Century: Resurrecting Urban America* (New York: Rowman & Littlefield Publishers, Inc., 1999).

22. "America's Best Hospitals: Psychiatry," *U.S. News and World Report*, 17 July 2000, 107; "America's Best Colleges 2000: Best National Universities," *U.S. News and World Report*, 30 August 1999, 88.

Chapter 5

1. Organization for Economic Co-operation and Development, *Education at a Glance: 2000 Edition* (Paris: OECD, 2000), Chart C2.1, p. 138; and Chart C3.1, p. 150.

2. Reference here is to proportions; that is, even if the total educational budget is greatly increased, the need to change the relative proportions accorded to various parts will still stand.

3. For more discussion, see Amitai Etzioni, *The Spirit of Community* (New York: Touchstone, 1993).

4. Matt Kempner, "The Big Wink," *Atlanta Journal and Constitution,* 23 January 2000, 1A.

5. Ibid.; Louis Freedberg, "Borderline Hypocrisy," *Washington Post,* 6 February 2000, B1; Dave Harmon, "Don't Ask, Don't Tell: Austin's Red Hot Economy Relies Heavily on Illegal Immigrants," *Austin American-Statesman,* 5 December 1999.

6. U.S. Immigration and Naturalization Service, "Illegal Alien Resident Population," 1999. Available at http://www.ins.usdoj.gov/graphics/aboutins/statistics/illegalalien/index.htm. Accessed on 3 July 2000. This figure was updated on the basis of discussion with Robert Warren at the Immigration and Naturalization Service on 3 May 2000.

7. "The Condition of Education 1997," Indicator 45. Available at http://nces.ed.gov/pubs/ce/c9745a01.html. Accessed on 3 July 2000.

8. For a review of the relative merits of different ways of introducing immigrant children to the English language, see J. David Ramirez, Sandra D. Yuen, and Dena R. Ramey, "Executive Summary of the Final Report: Longitudinal Study of Structured English Immersion Strategy, Early-Exit, and Late-Exit Transitional Bilingual Education Programs for Language-Minority Children," February 1991. Available at http://www.ncbe.gwu.edu/miscpubs/ramirez/longitudinal.htm. Accessed on 3 July 2000. Note that the study cited takes into account only the effects on immigrant children and not on other children or on the teachers.

9. National Council of La Raza, "Background and Talking Points on the President's English Language and Civics Education Initiative, and the Sample Letter to Congress About This Initiative, English Language and Civics Education Initiative: Common Ground Partnerships." Available at http://www.nifl.gov/nifl-esl/1999/0625.html. Accessed on 1 July 2000.

10. Ibid.

11. Ellen Summerfield, *Survival Kit for Multicultural Living* (Yarmouth, Maine: Intercultural Press, Inc., 1997), 29.

12. The Empowerment Network, an organization comprised of legislators, grassroots organizers, and other civic leaders, has advocated a similar idea through matched saving and investment accounts called Individual Development Accounts (IDAs).

13. Amitai Etzioni and Laura Brodbeck, *The Intergenerational Covenant: Rights and Responsibilities* (Washington, D.C.: The Communitarian Network, 1995).

14. U.S. Department of Labor, "The Employment Situation: April 2000," May 2000.

15. Gary Burtless suggested a similar idea but argued that they should pay less than the minimum wage, in "Growing American Equality," in Henry J. Aaron and Robert D. Reischauer, eds., *Setting National Priorities: The 2000 Election and Beyond* (Washington, D.C.: Brookings Institution Press, 1999), 160.

16. Robert H. Bork, "There's No Choice: Dismember Microsoft," *Wall Street Journal*, 1 May 2000, A34.

Chapter 6

1. Personal communication.

2. Although under some conditions public officials are reimbursed for "reasonable" legal fees, they might not receive such reimbursement until years later. Moreover, if they are not exonerated, if the prosecutor merely closes the case, no reimbursement is forthcoming, as is the case for President Clinton. And if relatives and friends of those investigated are summoned–often as a way to pressure the number one suspect–they are stuck with their bills, as was the case for several people in the social circle of former Housing and Urban Development secretary Henry Cisneros.

3. Quoted in Joan Biskupic, "News Analysis: From Nixon to Clinton," *Washington Post*, 1 June 1997, C1.

4. Quoted in Linda Greenhouse, "Word for Word: The Justices and Paula Jones," *New York Times*, 15 March 1998, sec. 4, p. 1.

5. Quoted in ibid.

6. Akhil Reed Amar, "The Unimperial Presidency," *New Republic*, 8 March 1999, 34.

7. Ibid., 41.

8. William Safire, "After Indy Counsels," *New York Times*, 4 March 1999, A25.

9. Quoted in "The Testing of a President: Excerpts from Minority Counsel Presentation to House Judiciary Committee," *New York Times*, 6 October 1998, A23.

10. Quoted in ibid.

11. Quoted in ibid.

12. Quoted in "The President's Trial," *New York Times*, 17 January 1999, sec. 1, p. 30.

13. Gerald R. Ford, statements before the 105th Congress, 2nd sess., *Congressional Record* (9 September 1998).

14. Robert Byrd, statements before the 105th Congress, 2nd sess., *Congressional Record* (9 September 1998).

15. Eric Pianin, "Senators Exploring a Form of Censure Are Bumping into Obstacles," *Washington Post*, 28 January 1999, A17; Associated Press, "Debate Moderator Known for Fairness," *Minneapolis Star Tribune*, 10 December 1998, 7A.

16. Paul C. Light and Virginia L. Thomas, *The Merit and Reputation of an Administration: Presidential Appointees on the Appointment Process*, for the Presidential Appointee Initiative (Washington, D.C.: The Brookings Institution, 28 April 2000), 8.

17. Ibid., 12.

18. Paul C. Light, "Battle of the Bureaus," *Washington Post*, 11 March 1999, A31.

19. Task Force on Presidential Appointments, "Obstacle Course: Report of the Task Force on the Presidential Appointment and Senate Confirmation Process" (Washington, D.C.: Century Foundation, September1996), 23.

20. Norma Holloway Johnson, *Re Grand Jury Proceedings*, Misc. Action No. 98-095, U.S. District Court for the District of Columbia, 26 May 1998.

21. Paul E. Begala, "Democrats Play the Vengeance Game," *New York Times*, 10 May 2000, A31.

22. Deborah Tannen, *The Argument Culture: Moving from Debate to Dialogue* (New York: Random House, 1998).

23. Joyce Ladner, an African American and outstanding social scientist and public activist, called for the African American community to frame issues in ways that facilitate nonracial coalition building. See Joyce Ladner, "A New Civil Rights Agenda," *Brookings Review* 18, no. 2 (Spring 2000): 26–28.

24. See Elizabeth Drew, *The Corruption of American Politics: What Went Wrong and Why* (Woodstock, N.Y.: Overlook Press, 2000); John B. Judis, *Paradox of American Democracy: Elites, Special Interests, and the Betrayal of the Public Trust* (New York: Pantheon Books, 2000).

25. Lisa Klein, "On the Brink of Reform: Political Party Funding in Britain," *Case Western Reserve Journal of Law* 31 (Winter 1999): 1–46.

26. Ibid.

27. Ibid.

28. Walter Shapiro, "Taxpayers Pick Up Tab of the Campaign Pipers," *USA Today*, 15 May 1996, 5A; Don Van Natta Jr., "A $3 Billion Record, but Does Anyone Care?" *New York Times*, 23 January 2000, D1.

Chapter 7

1. Arthur M. Schlesinger Jr., *The Disuniting of America: Reflections on a Multicultural Society* (New York: W. W. Norton and Co., 1998).

2. Betty Friedan, *Beyond Gender: The New Politics of Work and Family* (Washington, D.C.: Woodrow Wilson Center Press, 1997).

3. Richard W. Riley, "Secretary's Statement on Religious Expression," U.S. Department of Education Release to Educators, June 1998. Available at http://www.ed.gov/Speeches/08-1995/religion.html. Accessed on 14 August 2000.

4. Andrew Hacker, *Two Nations: Black and White, Separate, Hostile, Unequal* (New York: Ballantine Books, 1995).

5. For much more discussion, see Amitai Etzioni, *The Monochrome Society* (Princeton: Princeton University Press, forthcoming).

6. Robert Z. Lawrence, "Inequality in America: The Recent Evidence," *The Responsive Community* 10, no. 2 (Spring 2000): 4–10.

7. Eugene Steuerle from the Urban Institute, quoted in Jodie T. Allen, "Why the Tax Issue Can't Get Traction," *U.S. News and World Report*, 24 April 2000, 30.

8. Ted Halstead, "The Big Tax Bite You Don't Even Think About," *Washington Post*, 23 April 2000, B5.

9. Allen, "Why the Tax Issue Can't Get Traction," 30.

10. Isaac Shapiro and Robert Greenstein, *The Widening Gulf* (Washington, D.C.: Center on Budget and Policy Priorities, September 1999).

11. Isabel V. Sawhill, "Still the Land of Opportunity?" *The Public Interest* 135 (Spring 1999): 3–17.

12. Michael Sherraden, *Assets and the Poor: A New American Welfare Policy* (New York: M. E. Sharpe, Inc., 1991).

13. For details, see "IRS Audits Target the Working Poor; Congress Wanted Crackdown on Abuse of Low-Income Tax Credit," *St. Louis Post-Dispatch*, 16 April 2000, A10.

14. Executive Office of the President of the United States, Budget of the United States Government, Fiscal Year 2001 (Washington, D.C.: U.S. Government Printing Office, 2000).

15. The reference here is not primarily to items that are "paid for" by having to watch ads; in this sense TV is also a "free" good. The reference is especially to items such as Pretty Good Privacy, a software that allows people to protect their messages by encrypting them and that was put on the Internet by a scholar, completely free of charge.

Chapter 8

1. Frank M. Andrews and Stephen B. Withey, *Social Indicators of Well-Being: Americans' Perceptions of Life Quality* (New York: Plenum Press, 1976), 254–255.

2. Jonathan L. Freedman, *Happy People: What Happiness Is, Who Has It, and Why* (New York: Harcourt Brace Jovanovich, 1978).

3. David G. Myers and Ed Diener, "Who Is Happy?" *Psychological Science* 6 (January 1995): 12–13. See also Robert E. Lane, *The Market Experience* (Cambridge: Cambridge University Press, 1991), chapter 26.

4. Abraham Maslow, *Toward a Psychology of Being*, 3rd ed. (John Wiley and Sons, 1998); Amitai Etzioni, "Alienation, Inauthenticity, and Their Reduction," in *The Active Society* (New York: Free Press, 1968), 617–654.

5. Robert Fogel, *The Fourth Great Awakening and the Future of Egalitarianism* (Chicago: University of Chicago Press, 1999).

6. This position was articulated by Senator Joe Lieberman in the 2000 election campaign.

7. Social scientists differ on this point. See Robert Wuthnow, *Rediscovering the Sacred: Perspectives on Religion in Contemporary Society* (Grand Rapids, Mich.: William B. Eerdmans Publishing Co., 1992). For further discussion of recent American religious life, see Wuthnow, *The Restructuring of American Religion: Society and Faith Since World War II* (Princeton, NJ, Princeton University Press, 1988), and *After Heaven: Spirituality in America Since the 1950s* (Berkeley and Los Angeles: University of California Press, 1998).

8. Margaret Talbot, "A Mighty Fortress," *New York Times*, 27 February 2000, sec. 6, p. 34.

9. For additional discussion, see Amitai Etzioni, "Voluntary Simplicity: Characterization, Select Psychological Implications, and Societal Consequences," *Journal of Economic Psychology* 19, no. 5 (October 1998): 619–643. Some voluntary simplicity might be bogus, at least in the sense that it is fashionable to simplify, even if it costs a great deal. See David Brooks, *Bobos in Paradise* (New York: Simon and Schuster, 2000).

10. For more on this point, see Myron Magnet, *The Dream and the Nightmare: The Sixties' Legacy to the Underclass* (New York: William Morrow, 1993).

11. Robert Bellah et al., *Habits of the Heart: Individualism and Commitment in American Life* (Berkeley and Los Angeles: University of California Press, 1985).

Acknowledgments

I am indebted to David Boldt, Jessica Einhorn, John B. Judis, Elizabeth Rose, and Isabelle Sawhill for comments on a previous draft; to Jennifer Ambrosino, Mary Wilson, Natalie Klein, and Rachel Mears for editorial assistance; and to Jason Marsh and Joanna Cohn for research assistance. In particular, I benefited from extensive and elaborate fine editorial comments and suggestions by Tim Bartlett. A rather different version of this book was published by Demos in Britain.

Index

129